W9-ANI-738

Simple

KNITTING

Creative Makers

Simple
KNITTING

30 Quick-to-Knit Projects for Stylish Accessories

Ros Badger

PHOTOGRAPHY BY YUKI SUGIURA • DESIGNED BY ANITA MANGAN

Mitchell Beazley

Simple Knitting by Ros Badger

An Hachette UK Company
www.hachette.co.uk

First published in Great Britain in 2013 by
Mitchell Beazley, a division of Octopus Publishing Group Ltd
Endeavour House
189 Shaftesbury Avenue
London
WC2H 8JY
www.octopusbooks.co.uk
www.octopusbooksusa.com

Copyright © Octopus Publishing Group Ltd 2013

Distributed in the US by
Hachette Book Group USA
237 Park Avenue
New York NY 10017 USA

Distributed in Canada by
Canadian Manda Group
165 Dufferin Street
Toronto, Ontario, Canada M6K 3H6

ISBN 978 1 84533 696 7

A CIP catalogue record for this book is available from the
British Library

Printed and bound in China

10 9 8 7 6 5 4 3 2 1

Publisher: Alison Starling
Senior Art Editor: Juliette Norsworthy
Design: Anita Mangan
Assistant Designer: Abigail Read
Editors: Alex Stetter & Katy Denny
Copy editing: Lydia Darbyshire
Pattern checking: Marilyn Wilson
Photography: Yuki Sugiura
Styling: Cynthia Inions
Assistant Production Manager: Caroline Alberti

CONTENTS

THE PROJECTS

INTRODUCTION

When asked what I wanted to be when I grew up, I would always answer 'a fashion designer', as I loved drawing and making clothes from a very early age. I was brought up in a family where sewing and knitting were a way of life: my mum, grandmother and aunty were always making something, or so it seemed. Consequently, I was taught to knit and crochet at the age of eight. I remember taking a blanket I was making for my dolly's cot with me to primary school so I could work on it at lunchtime, so obsessed was I with finishing it.

I started making clothes for my dolls and teddy bears, and then progressed to designing and sewing my own clothes as a teenager. This may make me sound like someone from a bygone era, but I was brought up in 1960s and '70s Liverpool, and being able to sew and knit meant simply being able to wear the latest fashion trends. I appreciate how lucky I was to be taught useful skills at such an early age and that my childhood interests were nurtured. I'm even luckier to have made a career out of doing something I love: I don't count myself as a fashion designer in the true sense, but I haven't strayed very far from my original passion.

After studying textile design at Chelsea College of Art, I worked as a freelance knitwear designer for various companies and fashion designers, including Marks & Spencer and Betty Jackson, creating distinctive machine-knitted pieces. I also designed my own collection of women's and men's hand knits which were sold in Europe and the United States, and I employed artisan knitters across the UK to make up many of my

designs. While that tradition has died away, in its place are new knitters like you, dear reader, keen to create pieces for yourself, inspired by the plethora of beautiful patterns and yarns available and learning skills that you can pass on and share with family and friends, as has always been the way. Knitting is a craft that goes back thousands of years, but while it started as a way of making socks, stockings and other warm, practical garments, it now also plays a huge part in fashion. These days, you can find yarns of any hue, thickness and texture to create your own designer wear.

My main design influence was and still is the period from the 1920s to the 1950s, a time when knitting was en vogue and designs were incredibly creative, most likely because making things oneself was the only way to possess the latest style of cardigan,

knitted dress or even underwear. I have a huge collection of vintage knitting patterns, which I often look to for inspiration in my work – some of them inspired the designs in this book. My two teenaged daughters also influence my design decisions, giving me ideas and feedback. They both have an appreciation of handmade and vintage clothes too, which probably started when they were toddlers and I made them wear 'real' clothes with buttons instead of Velcro! Whether this was right or wrong I don't know, but I'm glad to say they have turned out OK.

It may be a cliché, but when I had my first daughter, Martha, my design interests shifted and for a number of years, I created a range of children's knitwear under the label Little Badger. My youngest daughter is also a teenager now, but I still think of both of them

as my muses. By designing pieces with them in mind, I feel as if I am creating my own traditions while keeping in touch with modern trends.

I like to think that we are entering a golden age of making, where knitting, crochet, sewing and crafting are now seen as being super cool; a wonderful way of expressing your individuality and creativity. When the world can often be fast and furious, filled with ever-changing technologies, the 'making' traditions bring us back down to earth. It feels good to make things for ourselves and our loved ones. Not too long ago many traditional skills looked like they were disappearing from everyday life, but now they are firmly back. I'm not sure whether this is a backlash against consumerism or a reaction to the recession:

whatever the reason, I couldn't be happier about the return of knitting as a popular pastime as I have been extolling its virtues for as long as I can remember. So I was overjoyed to be able to create a range of knitting patterns for the modern maker, using a gorgeous selection of yarns, from lace and mohair to chunky wool. This book offers something for everyone, with patterns suitable for absolute beginners and fresh ideas for old-school knitters. I sincerely hope it inspires you to pick up your needles and get knitting.

For more about me go to www.rosbadger.com and follow me on Twitter @rosbadger.

KNITTING ESSENTIALS

I find that keeping all my knitting and crochet materials in one place makes life easier, especially when you need to find something in a hurry. Much of the same equipment is needed for both crafts, so I store everything together in an old wooden sewing box. However, a knitting bag is also a useful thing to have, as you can keep your work-in-progress safe in it and carry it with you.

Apart from the essentials listed here, I find a button box to be a real asset, as I like to use old buttons to give projects an individual look. A selection of small scraps and ends of knitting yarn for embroidery or darning is also useful – keep them safe in a pretty tin or bag. And finally, it's always a good idea to keep pencil and paper to hand, for making tension/gauge calculations and keeping track of where you are in your work.

Knitting needle conversion chart

Metric	US	British (UK)
2 mm	0	14
2.5 mm	1	13
2.75 mm	2	12
3mm	n/a	11
3.25 mm	3	10
3.5 mm	4	n/a
3.75 mm	5	9
4 mm	6	8
4.5 mm	7	7
5 mm	8	6
5.5 mm	9	5
6 mm	10	4
6.5 mm	10.5	3
7 mm	n/a	2
7.5 mm	n/a	1
8 mm	11	0
9 mm	13	0
10 mm	15	0

- **A selection of knitting needles in a variety of sizes,** I keep most of mine in an old stoneware jar, but some are in fabric rolls, like those shown on page 9. Most people find metal needles the easiest to knit with, but some prefer plastic or bamboo.
- **Circular needles,** where the hard tips are joined by a flexible cord, for knitting round projects. These are also great for knitting heavier items, as you don't have to support the whole weight of the work by your hands.
- **A cable needle** – the 'bend' keeps your stitches safe when knitting cables.
- **A set of double-pointed needles,** for making cables or knitting in the round.
- **Needle gauge,** very useful for checking the sizes of double-pointed or circular needles, which are often only marked on the package.
- **Various crochet hooks of different sizes** – handy for finishing off projects with crochet edges or picking up dropped stitches.
- **A tape measure.**
- **Small, sharp scissors** – embroidery scissors are perfect.
- **Stitch holder** for holding stitches when changing needles. You can also use a double-pointed needle or a length of yarn instead.
- **Safety pins** of various sizes, useful for threading cords and keeping small numbers of stitches safely together.
- **Straight pins** with coloured heads so that they don't get lost in your knitting.
- **Tapestry/darning needles,** for sewing pieces of knitting together.

Straight knitting needles

Tape measure

Double-pointed needle

Stitch holder

Cable needle

Circular needles

Needle gauge

Safety pins

Crochet hook

Small, sharp scissors

Tapestry/darning needle

Straight pin

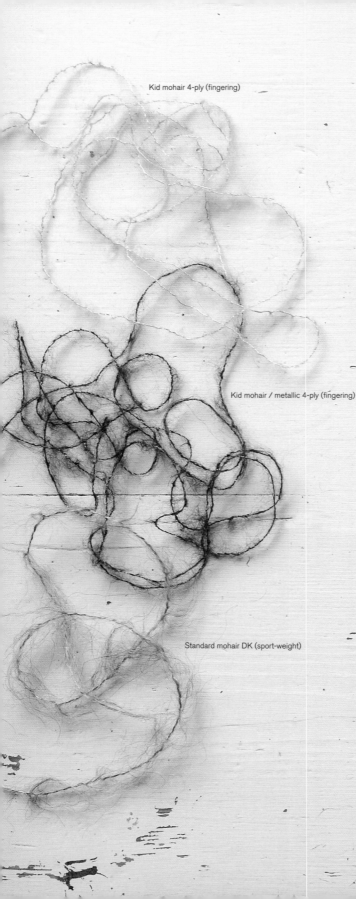

Kid mohair 4-ply (fingering)

Kid mohair / metallic 4-ply (fingering)

Standard mohair DK (sport-weight)

CHOOSING YARN

I try to stick to natural fibres such as wool, cotton and silk for most of my designs, as I believe that when you are spending time making something by hand, you should want the best results, and good-quality yarn will last longer, keep its shape and wash well. Cotton obviously has different qualities to wool – for one thing it's less elastic, making it a little trickier to knit with – but as a rule of thumb, natural is best.

There are five basic types of smooth yarn, categorized by weight: from lightest to heaviest, they are 4-ply (fingering), double-knitting or DK (sport-weight), Aran (worsted weight), chunky (bulky) and super chunky (super bulky). The finer the yarn, the smaller the needles – most ball bands will suggest a suitable needle size and a tension/gauge guide.

Although I recommend specific yarns for the projects in this book, it is of course not essential to use the exact materials specified: if a yarn is discontinued or hard to find, choose an alternative – yarn weight is defined the same way by all manufacturers, so an Aran-weight (worsted-weight) yarn should be the same thickness, no matter the producer. As long as the tension/gauge matches, then the pattern should work out (for more on achieving the correct tension/gauge, see page 35). However, when selecting yarn for any pattern, it is important to make sure that the type of yarn is appropriate, too: if you use 4-ply (fingering) mohair where 4-ply (fingering) mercerised cotton is recommended, the results will not be the same.

You may also find that buying yarn on a cone rather than in balls is more economical, and discontinued yarn shades are often available for good prices on yarn suppliers' websites and online auction sites. I have listed some of these on page 141.

Extra-fine merino wool 3-ply (lace-weight)

Wool 4-ply (fingering)

Cotton 4-ply (fingering)

Wool DK (sport-weight)

Wool Aran (worsted weight)

Wool Aran (worsted weight)

Wool chunky (bulky)

Wool tweed chunky (bulky)

ABBREVIATIONS

alt	alternate
beg	begin/beginning
cm	centimetre/centimetres
cont	continue
dec	decrease/decreasing
DK	double knitting
dpn	double-pointed needle
foll	follow/follows/following
in	inch/inches
inc	increase/increasing
K	knit
Kfb	knit into the front and then into the back of the same stitch to make 2 stitches
K2tog	knit 2 stitches together
M1	pick up bar between 2 stitches and knit through back loop
mm	millimetres
oz	ounce/ounces
P	purl
patt	pattern
P2tog	purl 2 stitches together
psso	pass slipped stitch over
rem	remain/remaining
rep	repeat/repeated
RS	right side
sl	slip
sl1	pass 1 stitch across to other needle without working
sl2Kpo	slip 2 stitches on to the right-hand needle as if knitting 2 together, knit 1, then pass the 2 slipped stitches over
ssk	slip, slip, knit (see page 24)
st/sts	stitch/stitches
st st	stocking/stockinette stitch
tbl	through back of loop/loops
tog	together
WS	wrong side
yf	yarn forward
yo/yon	yarn over needle (see page 22)
yrn	yarn round needle (see page 22)
[ ]and *	repeat instructions between brackets or after asterisks as many times as instructed

CASTING ON

The first step in any knitting project is casting on the required number of stitches. There are several different methods of casting on – the two shown here both start with a simple slip knot.

Making a slip knot

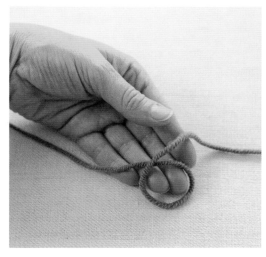

1 Casting on starts with making a slip knot. Make a loop with your yarn, passing the right side over the left.

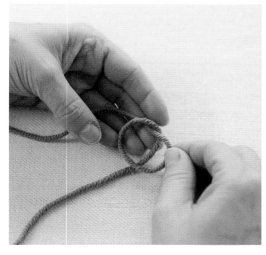

2 Using the tail end, pull a second loop though the first.

3 Adjust the loop to the correct size by pulling the tail end.

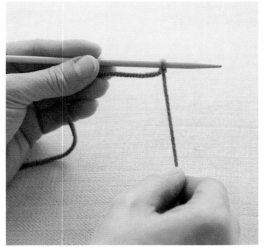

4 Place the slip knot on the left-hand (LH) needle – this forms the first stitch.

Casting on: Simple method

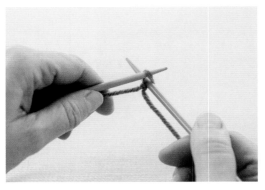

1 Pass the right-hand (RH) needle upwards through the slip knot on the LH needle.

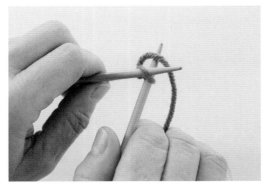

2 Pass the wool from the back to front of the RH needle ...

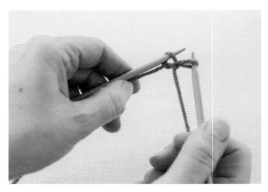

3 ... and draw through the stitch on to the LH needle, forming a loop.

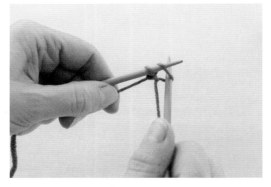

4 Slip the new loop on to the LH needle. There are now two stitches on the needle.

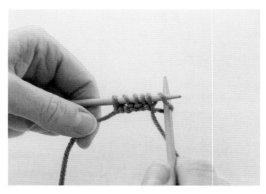

5 Repeat these steps until you have the required number of stitches.

Casting on: Cable method

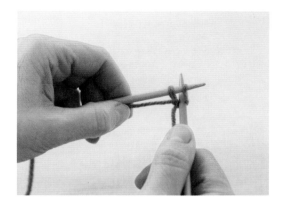

1 Place the slip knot on the left-hand (LH) needle, then make one more stitch as described in the method opposite. To make the third stitch, instead of passing the RH needle upwards through the loop of the last stitch, pass it between the two stitches.

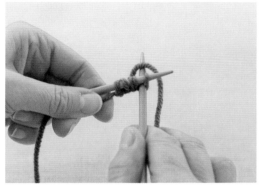

2 Wrap the yarn around the point of the RH needle …

3 … and draw it through the loop formed between the two stitches.

4 Slip the new stitch on to the LH needle.

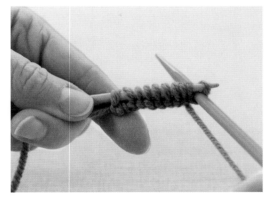

5 Proceed in this way, always working between the stitches instead of through them, until you have the required number of stitches.

BASIC STITCHES: KNIT & PURL

I find it reassuring to know that all knitting stitch patterns are made up of two basic stitches, knit and purl; the combination of these stiches and the direction of the yarn over the needle defines the various textures and patterns, from moss/seed stitch to lace and cables. Once you learn these two basic stitches you will soon find that you will be able to achieve any number of patterns. Most knitters find the knit stitch very easy and the purl slightly harder but once

mastered the method seems to become imprinted on the mind. I love this quote from knitter Martha Waterman: 'Given good yarn, good workmanship, and good care, a knitted shawl can outlive its knitter, providing warmth and pleasure to several generations of family and friends'. I would advise that we all apply this to our knitting: start your work with good intent, use the best quality yarn that you can afford and make up your work with the same care as you pay to the knitting of it.

Knit stitch

Plain knitting, most commonly called garter stitch, is when you work every row in knit stitch. Both the right side (RS), meaning the side that will be on show when the piece is

worn, and wrong side (WS) of the knitting will look the same, with wavy horizontal ridges. When working the knit stitch, you always keep the yarn at the back of the work.

1 Hold the needle with the stitches in your left hand and the other needle and the yarn in your right. Insert the right-hand (RH) needle from left to right through the first stitch.

2 Pass the yarn between both points of the needles.

3 Draw the loop through to the front with the RH needle, pulling the left needle under the right.

4 Keeping the tension with your fingers, slip the stitch off the LH needle and on to the RH needle.

5 Continue in this way until all the stitches on your LH needle are knitted, then change the needles to the opposite hands and continue.

Purl stitch

Purl stitch is worked with the yarn at the front – think of it like working a knit stitch backwards. If you purl every row, the knitting will look like garter stitch, but by knitting on the right-side rows and purling on the wrong-side rows, you create stocking/stockinette stitch: on the right side, the stitches form little 'V' shapes and the fabric is smooth, while the wrong side looks like garter stitch. Stocking/stockinette stitch does tend to curl up, so will need careful steaming or blocking (see page 31).

The purl rows usually form the wrong side of the work, unless otherwise specified. When the purl side is used as the right side, the stitch will most likely be referred to as reverse stocking/stockinette stitch, as for example in the cable beret pattern on page 68.

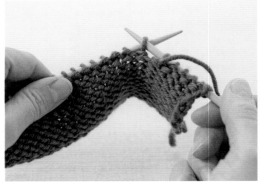

1 Work a knit row, then hold the needle with your stitches in the left hand, so that the wrong side of the work is facing you. Pass the right-hand (RH) needle through the front of the first stitch from right to left.

2 Pass the yarn over and around the point of the RH needle.

3 Draw the loop through the stitch to the back on the LH needle …

4 … and pass it to the RH needle, slipping the stitch off the LH needle. Repeat until all stitches have been worked.

TECHNIQUES & TEXTURES

With a few simple techniques, you will be able to shape your knitting by increasing and decreasing the number of stitches, create pretty lace patterns and cables and knit colourful stripes. It is worth remembering that all knitting stitch patterns are a combination of knit and purl stitch, and the vast number of textured stitches available are simply a combination of knit and purl.

Increasing

To increase the width of your knitting, you can make additional stitches by using an existing stitch as the base for a new stitch.

1 Insert the right-hand (RH) needle into the stitch, wrap the yarn around the needle and pull through as for a normal knit stitch, but lengthen the loop slightly, and don't pull the stitch off the LH needle yet.

2 Bring the tip of the RH needle around to the back and knit into the back of the loop.

3 Slip the stitch off the LH needle: you have made two stitches from one …

4 … and you now have an additional stitch on the RH needle.

Make one knit stitch (M1)

There are a number of different ways of adding more stitches to your knitting – you can also make a new stitch by knitting the bar or strand of yarn lying between two adjacent stitches.

1 With the left-hand (LH) needle, pick up the bar of yarn between two stitches from front to back. Use the RH needle to knit this bar through the back loop, so that an extra stitch is added to the RH needle.

Yarn/wool over needle (YO/YON or WON)

Wrapping the yarn over the needle (or making a yarn over) to create a loop can be another form of increase, this technique is also used in lace patterns: when the newly made loop is knitted in the next row, a little hole is created in the fabric of the knitting.

1 Simply pass the yarn over the right-hand (RH) needle, from back to front, before working the next stitch – this is usually done before a knit stitch. In the next row, work the new loop like a normal stitch.

In some lace patterns, the instruction to make a 'yarn over' (YON) is followed by the instruction to knit two stitches together (k2tog), to keep the number of stitches in the row consistent.

Yarn/wool round needle (YRN or WRN)

Very similar to yarn over needle (YO/YON), this technique is used on purl rows.

1 Pass the yarn over the right-hand (RH) needle, from front to back, before working the next stitch.

Knit two stitches together (K2tog)

The most common way to reduce your number of stitches – and thereby decrease the width of your knitting – is to knit two stitches together (K2tog). This type of decrease can be worked at any point in the fabric.

1 Insert the point of the right-hand (RH) needle through the 2 stitches to be decreased on the LH needle.

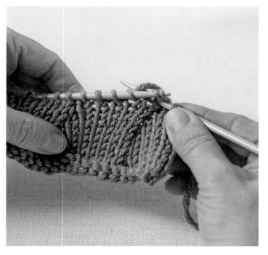

2 Wrap the yarn around the point of the RH needle …

3 … and draw 1 stitch through both of the stitches.

4 Slip the 2 stitches off the LH needle, making 1 stitch out of 2 on the RH needle.

Slip slip knit (SSK)

This is a basic way to decrease two stitches at once, and is usually made a few stitches in from the edge of your knitting.

1 Knit to the point where the decrease is to be made. Slip the first stitch as if to knit, slip the second stitch as if to knit, then slide the left-hand (LH) needle into the front part of both slipped stitches on the RH needle, wrap the yarn around the tip and pull through to knit them together.

2 As this decrease slants to the left, this technique is often paired with knit two together (K2tog), which makes a right-slanting decrease.

Pass slipped stitch over (PSSO)

This is another technique to use when decreasing your number of stitches, particularly when working lace patterns.

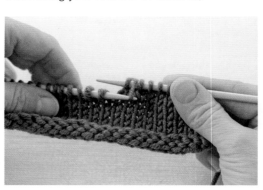

1 Using the point of the RH needle, slip the stitch from the LH needle to the RH needle, without working it. Work the stitch(es) over which the slipped stitch is to be passed. Then insert the point of the LH needle into the slipped stitch...

2 ...and pull it over the knit stitch(es), dropping it off the end of the RH needle.

Cable stitch

The rope-like twists of a classic cable pattern are easier to achieve than you might think: it's really nothing more than knitting a few stitches 'in the wrong order'. A cable is made by crossing one group of stitches over another, either at the back or in front of your work.

1 To make a right-twisting cable, slip 3 stitches on to the cable needle and keep them at the back of the work.

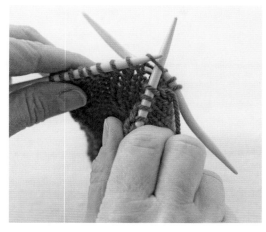

2 Knit 3 stitches from the left-hand (LH) needle.

3 Bring the cable needle forward and knit the 3 stitches from this needle.

4 Continue as per the pattern instructions. When knitting a standard cable, you usually cross stitches every sixth or eighth row on a RS row. To make a cable that twists to the left, hold 3 stitches on a cable needle in front of your work when knitting 3 stitches from the LH needle.

Knit through back loop (TBL)

Because you change the direction from which the needle enters the stitch, knitting through the back loop results in a twisted stitch – a simple but decorative effect.

1 Insert the right-hand (RH) needle into the next stitch on the LH needle through the back loop, wrap the yarn around the needle and continue as for a standard knit stitch.

....

Joining a new colour: knitting stripes

Stripes are a very simple and effective way of adding interest and colour to your knitting.

1 When you are ready to change colour, complete your row and cut the yarn, leaving a 10 cm (4 in) tail – you will weave this end into the work later. To add the second colour, leave a 10 cm (4 in) tail and hold the yarn tight, as when beginning a regular row, and start knitting. If you find this tricky, hold both the tail of the first yarn and the new yarn as you make the first stitch, being careful to only knit with the new colour.

2 If you are knitting thin stripes, only a couple of rows high, there is no need to cut and re-join the yarn after each stripe is finished: instead you can pass it up the side of your work when you're ready to use the colour again – this keeps your work looking neat and leaves you with fewer ends to sew in later.

Making a heel

The ankle socks on page 86 use the heel-shaping method illustrated below. The slouchy pair on page 82 are made differently and the heel shaping happens at either end of the work.

1 When you reach the instructions for the heel shaping work row 1. On row 2 slip 1 st purlwise from the beginning of row 2.

2 P2tog, turn (end of row 2). This is where the heel stitches meet the stitches from the rest of the sock. Note that the method used for Slouchy Socks creates a row of diagonal eyelet-type holes at the heel.

3 When you have made the heel it's time to 'turn', by picking up stitches along the edge of your work. Insert your needle through a loop at the side of the knitting, this will be the last stitch in a row.

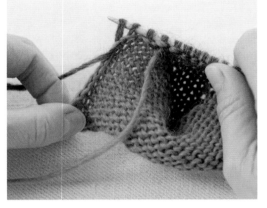

4 Pass your yarn over the needle and pull through the knitting to create a loop (or stitch) on the needle that will be worked on the return row. Follow the instructions, missing the rows specified to create an even tension/gauge.

FINISHING YOUR PROJECT

You've lavished time and attention on knitting your project, so it makes sense to devote the same amount of care on making up the finished item – you'll be glad you made the effort.

Casting (binding) off

When you have completed your piece of knitting, you need to cast/bind off your final row of stitches to prevent your work from unravelling.

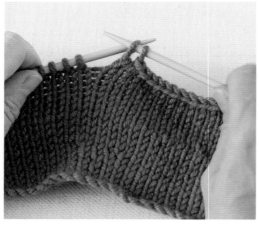

1 Knit 2 stitches. Pass the first stitch over the second stitch and off the needle. Knit another stitch so that there are 2 on the needle again. Pass the older stitch over the newer stitch and off the needle. Continue in this way …

2 … passing the older stitch over the newer and off the needle …

3 … then knitting another new stitch. Continue in this way until only 1 stitch remains. Cut the yarn and pass it through the last stitch, drawing the end up tightly to close the loop.

Weaving in ends

There is no right or wrong way here, other than making sure the ends are hidden and secured so that your work doesn't come undone. But here are some basic rules to follow to make things easier: when you're knitting, always start a new ball of yarn at the beginning of a row, never in the middle. Leave an end that's long enough to sew in but not so long that it will get in your way while knitting. However, if you want to use the end to sew up your seam later, leave a longer tail.

1 Any ends that you don't use to sew up your seams, weave horizontally or up or down a seam: thread your darning needle and weave the yarn through some of the stitches on the wrong side of your work, weaving through the purl loops.

2 Weave for a few centimetres (an inch or so), then carefully trim off the end of the yarn.

3 Where two colours meet, weave the end along the join ...

4 ... then trim the end close to the knitting.

Blanket stitch

This is a great, simple stitch for finishing off your knitting with a decorative edging. Blanket stitch is basically a buttonhole stitch, but instead of the stitches sitting very close together they lie parallel, approximately 1 cm (½ in) apart – the distance between stitches will vary depending on the look that you want to achieve and the thickness of your yarn.

 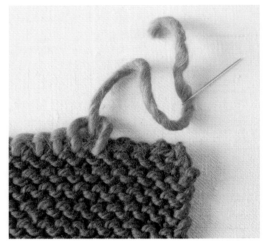

1 Thread a darning needle with a length of yarn, then push the needle through from back to front, about 1 cm (½ in) in from the edge of your work. Place your needle about 1 cm (½ in) along at the same level as the insertion point of the first stitch. Push the needle through, coming up through the loop you have created with the thread.

2 As you pull the thread gently through the loop you will see the first blanket stitch start to form. Finish the stitch off by pulling neatly but not tightly, then continue by placing the needle, front to back, 1 cm (½ in) along from the top of the last stitch and repeat.

Blocking and pressing

Handknitting tends to curl up, particularly if you're knitting in stocking/stockinette stitch. Before you sew up your seams, take the time to block or press your knitting so that the pieces will lie flat – it makes for much better results.

Blocking
Using rust-proof pins, pin the piece right-side up on your ironing board (you want a flat, padded surface), making sure the edges are straight and the shape is not distorted. If you've knitted socks or mittens, do not pin the ribbing. Spray the knitting with water, using a spray bottle, and leave it to dry completely before removing the pins. You can use a steam iron to block pieces knitted in natural fibres: cover your work with a dry cloth and hold the iron above it to let the steam penetrate the knitting.

Pressing
Pin your knitting to the ironing board as before, but with the wrong side up. Cover you work with a dry cloth and gently place the steam iron on the surface for a moment, then lift it off – do not slide it over the knitting as if you were ironing, but lift it off and place it down again. Let the knitting cool before removing it from the board.

JOINING SEAMS

The methods used when making up of your work are crucial. There is little point in knitting perfect pattern pieces if you then sew them together with wobbly stitches and seams. In most of my patterns I advise mattress stitch; it's fast and effective. Worked from the right side of the pieces, this method forms an invisible seam. Always follow a vertical line between two stitches to form the perfect seam. Backstitch is used when a firmer seam is needed or as an alternative to mattress stitch but be careful – if you make a mistake it can be difficult to undo.

Backstitch

This is a simple way to make a secure seam. Pin the two pieces together with right sides facing, making sure that their edges are even and any stripes or patterns line up. Pins should be at a right angle to the edge.

1 Thread a tapestry needle with the same yarn you used for your knitting and secure the yarn at theright-hand (RH) corner. Bring the needle up through both layers of knitting, one stitch in from the RH edge. Working from right to left, bring the needle back up again two stitches along from the previous stitch. Continue like this, going back over the previous stitch before making the next one.

2 On the reverse side, the stitches will overlap, while on the front, you will have a neat row of stitches meeting end to end. As you're sewing, try to maintain an even tension, and don't pull the stitches too tight – you want to keep your knitting flexible.

Mattress stitch

This method allows you to join two pieces knitted in stocking/stockinette stitch almost invisibly, by weaving between the stitches. If your pieces are the same size, you won't even need to use pins, as you will have the same number of rows on either side and they should match up perfectly. If the tail from your cast-on row is long enough, you can use this to sew up the seam.

1 Lay the pieces out flat with the right sides up and the edges parallel. Thread a tapestry needle with an end of yarn that matches your work – it should be about one and a half times the length of your seam – and fasten it to the bottom right-hand (RH) edge. Take the needle over to the LH side and insert it between the first and second stitches on the first row, bringing it up again 2 rows further up.

2 Pull gently to draw the edges together, then work the needle into the corresponding row on the RH side. Continue zig-zagging from side to side in this manner to make a flat, invisible seam.

If you find your pieces don't quite fit together, you can ease in the longer side by inserting the needle under three rows instead of two until the pieces match.

USEFUL TIPS

Keep a crochet hook in your kit and you need never panic if you drop a stitch – simply follow the instructions below. Once saved, your picked up stitch will blend in with the rest of your work.

Picking up a dropped stitch

If you drop a stitch, don't worry – you can easily get it back again.

1 With the right side of the knitting facing up, use a crochet hook to catch your dropped stitch.

2 Work your way back up the 'ladder' of loose strands above it, by hooking the next thread up and pulling it through the loop on your crochet hook.

3 When you reach the top of the ladder, slip the last stitch back on to your RH needle.

Placing a marker

When using a circular needle to make a continuous piece of knitting it can be very useful to place a stitch marker – a loop of cotton yarn in a contrast colour, fastened with a double knot – to remind you when to switch from knit to purl rows, or just to help you keep track.

1 Knit to where you want the marker to be, then slip it on the right-hand (RH) needle. Continue to knit stitches from the LH needle. When you reach the marker again, simply slip it from the LH needle to the RH needle, as you would a slip a stitch – this keeps the marker in the same position.

Tension/Gauge

Tension or gauge is the measurement of the tightness or looseness of the knitted fabric. On most yarn labels, you will see the recommended tension/gauge given in terms of the number of stitches and the number of rows over 10 cm (4 in) of stocking/stockinette stitch. Everyone knits differently, so to get the best results, it is important to knit a swatch and check your tension/gauge before you begin a project, even if you're using the yarn specified in the book. If your stitch and row counts are very different to those given, you will need to change your needles accordingly, otherwise your project will turn out larger or smaller than you intended.

1 Knit a swatch measuring at least 12 cm (5 in) square – it needs to be large enough so that you can accurately measure the number of stitches and rows over a 10 cm (4 in) square.
2 Flatten your knitting (you can steam press it or pin it to your ironing board) and mark out a 10 cm (4 in) square with pins.
3 Count the number of stitches and rows: if you have too many stitches and rows, your tension/gauge is too tight, so change to larger needles. If the number of stitches/ rows is fewer than that of the pattern, change to smaller needles.
4 Repeat the process, changing needles as appropriate, until your tension/gauge matches that of the pattern.

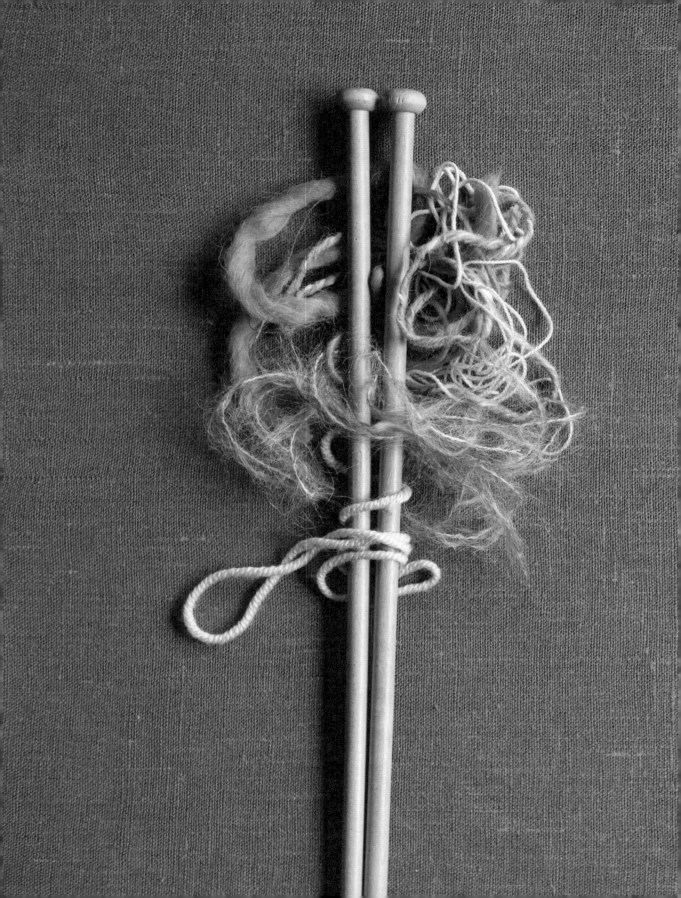

WRAP UP WARM

I often wear a scarf, not only on freezing, wintery days
but from early autumn onwards and into late spring, too.
With different textures and yarns, you can create something
for any occasion: this collection ranges from an effortlessly
elegant alpaca-silk muffler to a voluminous mohair cowl
that can double as a warm head scarf when you're out
on a long walk. There's a quirky but very practical
striped scarf with pockets, and a pretty scarf knitted
in a charming feathery lace stitch if you're looking
for something more delicate.

CHUNKY SCARF

This is an easy pattern for the novice knitter. It is made using garter stitch and thick yarn, which means that the scarf grows quickly, and it is possibly the simplest thing to make in this book. Once you have knitted the plain scarf, why not try one of the variations? I've provided a number of suggestions that are easy to achieve and will give you a completely different look. Add a fringe at each end for a cosy finish or use a contrast edging for a more sophisticated look. Once you feel confident, try knitting the striped scarf, experimenting with your own colour combinations.

YOU WILL NEED

4 × 100 g (3½ oz) balls of Rowan Big Wool in Forest (A); 1 × 100 g (3½ oz) ball in Vert (B)

Pair of 10 mm (US 15) knitting needles

TENSION/GAUGE

Using 10 mm (US 15) needles and working in garter st, 10 sts and 16 rows = 10 cm (4 in) square

FINISHED SIZE

144 × 30 cm (56½ × 12 in)

LEVEL

Starting out

METHOD

Plain scarf

With 10 mm (US 15) needles and A cast on 30 sts.
Row 1: Knit.
Row 2: Knit.
Rep rows 1–2 until the scarf measures 144 cm (56½ in) long or until you have used up all 4 balls of yarn. Cast/bind off.

To finish

Using B, work a blanket stitch edge at each end of the scarf. Sew in any loose ends.

Variations

Scarf with contrast edging

Work as for the plain scarf, but cast on in B, change to A to knit the scarf. Change to B to cast/bind off.

Striped scarf

You will need 1 × 100 g (3½ oz) ball of Rowan Big Wool in each of Wild Berry (A), Mulberry (B) and Linen (C). For a longer scarf, use 2 balls of each colour.

With 10 mm (US 15) needles and A cast on 30 sts.
Rows 1–2: Knit.
Change to B.
Rows 3–4: Knit.
Change to C.
Rows 5–6: Knit.
Rep Rows 1–6 until the scarf is 135 cm (53 in) long or until you have used up all the balls of yarn. Cast/bind off.

Scarf with fringed edging

Work as for the plain scarf. To make a fringed edging, cut 30 pieces of A, each 35 cm (13¾ in) long. Take one piece of yarn, fold it in half and thread the folded edge between the first and second stitches at the cast-on end of the scarf. Thread the two free ends through the loop to secure it to the scarf. Repeat with the remaining pieces of yarn, attaching a fringe piece between every other stitch along the cast-on edge. Repeat along the cast/bound-off edge. (See also page 56.)

FEATHER AND FAN STITCH LACY SCARF

Many of the vintage knitting patterns I have collected over the years use fine yarn, often 2-ply. I adore the lightness and look of fine yarn knitting – yes, it is slower to grow than a chunky knit, but the results are well worth the effort. Knitted in 4-ply (fingering) wool, this lacy scarf is light, smart and warm. I wear mine with my winter coat, and love the way that something so practical can also look so elegant.

For a look reminiscent of scarves from the 1930s and '40s, I have used a classic 'feather and fan' lace stitch. The pattern is worked over four rows, with the 'lace' produced on the third row: you work two stitches together, then make new stitches to form the holes. The pattern is easy to memorize, so once you get started you can work on your knitting wherever you are, without having to refer to the instructions.

For a strikingly different look, try working this lacy scarf in stripes: the different colours will follow the lines of the pattern to form waves, which can look fabulous in the right colours.

YOU WILL NEED

2 × 50 g (1¾ oz) balls of Debbie Bliss Rialto Lace in Sky

Pair of 2.75 mm (US 2) knitting needles

TENSION/GAUGE

Using 2.75 mm (US 2) needles and working in st st, 33 sts and 50 rows = 10 cm (4 in) square; this may vary when you are working in pattern

FINISHED SIZE

130 × 20 cm (51 × 7¾ in)

LEVEL

Going further

METHOD

With 2.75 mm (US 2) needles cast on 90 sts.
Row 1 (RS): Knit.
Row 2: Purl.
Row 3: *K2tog 3 times, [YO, K1] 6 times, K2tog 3 times*, rep from * to * 4 times more.
Row 4: Purl.
Rep rows 1–4 until work measures 130 cm (51 in), ending with a K row.
Cast/bind off.

To finish

Sew in any loose ends. Steam iron flat but without exerting too much pressure so that the pattern opens up but you do not stretch the scarf.

MAN'S TWEEDY SCARF

Not that long ago, a gentleman would always wear a hand-knitted scarf in winter. Today, most men will still wear a scarf when the weather turns cold but it's usually bought in a shop – if they're very lucky, it's a stylish designer knit, so here is an opportunity to make your own version for the fashionable man-about-town. Made of chunky, tweedy yarn, it would look just as good on a woman.

I have always had a fondness for tweed: it embodies quality and craftsmanship; it appeals to the retro side of my taste but is also currently enjoying something of a fashion revival. The lime green yarn I've chosen here feels masculine but with a bit of an edge, and makes for a great splash of colour against the greys, dark blues or blacks of men's outerwear. The pattern is another simple one, and the yarn is thick enough to ensure your scarf grows fast. I made mine 165 cm (65 in) long, but you can make yours shorter or longer, according to your own preferences. Just stop when it feels right to you.

YOU WILL NEED

5 × 50 g (1¾ oz) balls of Debbie Bliss Donegal Luxury Tweed Chunky in Apple

Pair of 6.5 mm (US 10½) knitting needles

TENSION/GAUGE

Using 6.5 mm (US 10½) needles and working in st st, 12 sts and 18 rows = 10 cm (4 in) square

FINISHED SIZE

165 × 22 cm (65 × 8½ in)

LEVEL

Starting out

METHOD

With 6.5 mm (US 10½) needles cast on 26 sts.
Rows 1–5: Work in garter st (K every row).
Row 6 (WS): K4, P18, K4.
Row 7: Knit.
Rep rows 6–7 until the work measures 163 cm (64 in), ending on a WS row. Work 5 rows in garter st. Cast/bind off knitwise.

To finish

Sew in any loose ends. Steam iron flat but without exerting too much pressure.

POCKET SCARF

A cosy wraparound scarf is a winter essential, but this one has a practical twist: pockets! Every year, we escape to Cornwall after Christmas with family and friends. There is no mobile phone reception at the house, and consequently our regular walks along the coast have turned into a welcome opportunity for the teenagers to check their messages whenever we find a signal en route. But where to put your phone? In the pocket of your scarf, of course!

The yarn is chunky, so even though the scarf is almost 2 metres (75 in) long, it grows very quickly. The mock rib stitch is a cinch, making this a perfect project for the new knitter. Of course you could ignore the striped section and knit this scarf in a single colour instead, or you could make your scarf shorter or a longer simply by reducing or increasing the number of rows between the pockets. So feel free to improvise: as long as you keep the pocket feature, you can't go wrong.

YOU WILL NEED

5 × 50 g (1¾ oz) balls of Debbie Bliss Rialto Chunky in Denim (A); 3 × 50 g (1¾ oz) balls in Duck Egg (B)

Pair of 6.5 mm (US 10½) knitting needles

TENSION/GAUGE

Using 6.5 mm (US 10½) needles and working in st st, 15 sts and 21 rows = 10 cm (4 in) square; this may vary when you are working in pattern

FINISHED SIZE

190 × 20.5 cm (75 × 8 in)

LEVEL

Moving on

NOTE

The first and last three stitches of each row are worked in garter stitch to stop the scarf from rolling in at the edges.

METHOD

With 6.5 mm (US 10½) needles and B cast on 31 sts.
Work 6 rows in garter st (K every row).
Change to A.
Row 1 (WS): K3, (P1, K1) to last 4 sts, P1, K3.
Row 2 (RS): Knit.
Rep Rows 1–2 until work measures 19 cm (7½ in) from cast-on edge, ending on a Row 1.
Cont from Row 1. (This is important because you are reversing the patt so that when the pocket is turned up the patt will continue to be on the RS of your work.)
Cont until work measures 59 cm (23¼ in) from cast-on edge, ending on a Row 1.
Change to B and cont in patt for 40 cm (15¾ in) more, ending on a Row 1.
Change to A and cont in patt for 30 cm (12 in) more, ending on a Row 1.

Change to B and cont in patt for 40 cm (15¾ in) more, ending on a Row 1.
Change to A and cont in patt for 40 cm (15¾ in) more.
The work should measure 209 cm (82¼ in).
Cont for 17 cm (6½ in) more, beg from Row 1 of patt. (This is for the turn-up of the pocket.) End on a Row 1.
Change to B and work 6 rows in garter st.
Cast/bind off knitwise.

To finish

Fold work 19 cm (7½ in) from cast-on edge to create pockets and sew with a neat overstitch on the RS of the work. Rep at the cast-off (bound-off) end. Sew in any loose ends.

SILKY MUFFLER

Knitted in moss/seed stitch, this muffler or throat warmer is another design born out of my obsession with vintage knitting patterns and my love of 1930s and '40s inspired fashion. While I don't have the original pattern for this muffler, I do have a picture of an elegant woman wearing a tight-fitting suit with a similar scarf tied at her neck, and I love it. The scarf in the picture looks as if it was knitted in garter stitch and considering the era, it was most likely made of wool, possibly lambswool if the wearer was very lucky. Either way, it wasn't nearly as luxurious as this design: the yarn is a mix of baby alpaca and mulberry silk, and a complete indulgence. It is fairly expensive but also very light, so this darling piece only uses one and a half balls of yarn. If you were to buy three, you could make a second muffler for a glamorous friend, which I'm sure would make you very popular.

The pattern starts with the rib and then works the moss/seed stitch either side so don't be confused by the instructions on Row 1. Also worth noting is that the rib is double thickness at one end of your work only, so that the opposite end can be passed through the double rib which gives the neckerchief appearance.

For a shorter muffler, or if you wanted to make up this design for a child, you simply knit fewer rows between the ribs. You could also follow this pattern using a DK (sport-weight) yarn for a different look.

YOU WILL NEED

2 × 50 g (1¾ oz) balls of Debbie Bliss Andes in Rose

Pair of 4 mm (US 6) knitting needles; 3.25 mm (US 3) double-pointed needle (dpn)

Darning needle

TENSION/GAUGE

Using 4 mm (US 6) needles and working in st st, 22 sts and 30 rows = 10 cm (4 in) square

FINISHED SIZE

70 × 15 cm (27½ × 6 in)

LEVEL

Going further

TIP

You could make two mufflers with 3 × 50 g (1¾ oz) balls.

METHOD

With 4 mm (US 6) needles cast on 15 sts. Beg with the rib section.

Row 1 (RS): [K1, P1] to last st, K1.

Row 2 (WS): [P1, K1] to last st, P1.

Rep Rows 1–2 four times more.

Row 11: As Row 1.

Row 12: Purl.

Row 13 (RS): [K1, M1] to last st, K1.

(29 sts)

**Work in moss (seed) st (every row is Row 1) for 25 rows.

Dec as foll:

Row 1 (RS): P2tog, moss/seed st to last 2 sts, P2tog tbl.

Row 2 (WS): K2tog tbl, moss/seed st to last 2 sts, K2tog.

Rep Rows 1–2 of dec until 3 sts remain.

Next row: Sl1, K2tog, psso.

Cut the yarn, leaving a few cm (approx 1 in), thread through the loop, then, using a tapestry needle, securely weave the end into the sts up and down so that it cannot work loose.**

Return to Row 12 (WS): Pick up and K 15 sts from the loops.

Starting with a WS row, [P1, K1] to last st, P1.

Work 10 rows in rib as set.

Make sure that you can identify the 15 original cast-on loops and slip them on to a small dpn. Knit tog 1 st and 1 loop across the row. (15 sts)

Next row: [K1, M1] to last st, K1. (29 sts)

Work in moss/seed st for 42 cm (16½ in) or less if making for a child.

Next row (RS): [K2tog, P2tog] to last st, K1. (15 sts)

Work 9 rows in rib, then, with RS facing, [K1, M1] to last st, K1. (29 sts)

Rep from ** to **.

Sew in any loose ends securely.

MOHAIR COWL

This pattern is very simple but so effective that people might not believe you've made this soft, flattering cowl yourself. The photograph shows it looped around the neck twice but it's long enough to wrap around three times for a snugger appearance – play around with it to see what works best for you. Knitted in fluffy mohair, this cowl makes a wonderful accessory for a plain coat or jacket. You could also use a smooth yarn, if you prefer, or even knit a striped version using a different colour every few rows.

This cowl is knitted in one piece using a circular needle. Casting on 180 stitches may seem daunting, but the piece grows very quickly, despite the number of stitches – you will only work approximately 40 rows, so it really doesn't take that long to make. To give it some body and stop it from curling at the edges, this cowl is knitted in garter stitch. However, when using a circular needle, this means alternating between knit and purl rows, so add a marker in a contrasting yarn to indicate where each round begins, as described on page 35.

YOU WILL NEED

130 g (4½ oz) Texere Destiny in Silver (from a cone)

6.5 mm (US 10½) and 6 mm (US 10) circular needles

TENSION/GAUGE

Using a 6 mm (US 10) circular needle and working in garter st, 11 sts and 20 rows = 10 cm (4 in) square

FINISHED SIZE

164 × 21 cm (64½ × 8¼ in)

LEVEL

 Starting out

TIPS

The cowl is knitted in garter stitch, so you should alternate a knit row with a purl row when you are using a circular needle.

When knitting a piece of this length, it can be useful to add a marker every 60 stitches, so you can count your stitches occasionally to make sure you're still on track.

METHOD

With a 6.5 mm (US 10½) circular needle cast on 180 sts. Change to a 6 mm (US 10) circular needle.
Round 1: Knit, adding a marker every 60 sts (use a smooth yarn in a contrasting colour). Add a third marker at the end of the first round to remind you when to change from knit to purl.
Round 2: Purl.
Rep Rounds 1–2 until work measures 21 cm (8¼ in).
Cast/bind off using a 6.5 mm (US 10½) circular needle.

To finish
Sew in the ends.

SIMPLE MOHAIR SCARF

This is the simplest of knits but the mohair yarn ensures that the finished scarf looks effortlessly elegant and stylish. Wear it loose or wrap it around your neck a couple of times for a cosy look. It's the perfect beginners' project as very little knitting knowledge is required to produce an eye-catching fashion piece.

The fine yarn is worked on largish needles, meaning that the scarf grows quickly, and the sparkly filaments help make this every bit the must-have accessory. Once you've completed your first scarf, you will be desperate to knit another one, or will have the confidence to move on and try your skills on a new project.

YOU WILL NEED

1 × 50 g (1¾ oz) ball of Debbie Bliss Party Angel in Saffron

Pair of 5.5 mm (US 9) knitting needles

TENSION/GAUGE

Using 5.5 mm (US 9) needles and working over garter st, 17 sts = 10 cm (4 in) and 25 rows; the row tension/gauge will vary from knitter to knitter

FINISHED SIZE

90 × 28 cm (35½ × 11 in)

LEVEL

Starting out

TIP

If you were to knit for only 80 cm (31½ in) you might be able to make two scarves from a 50 g (1¾ oz) ball of yarn.

METHOD

With 5.5 mm (US 9) needles cast on 48 sts.
Row 1: Knit.
Rep Row 1 (that is, work in garter stitch) until work measures 90 cm (35½ in). Cast/bind off.

To finish

Sew in any loose ends.

I spotted this fun idea in one of the many vintage children's knitting pattern books I have collected over the years. This type of hooded scarf was popular in the 1950s: making a hat and scarf in one not only saves time, but where children are concerned it also means there is one less item to lose. My daughters loved this idea when I showed it to them, and the fact that they thought this style was cool was enough for me to follow my instincts and make a 'grown-up' version for this book.

Moss/seed stitch is a favourite of mine. It is often used as an edging stitch because it lies so beautifully flat, but as an all-over subtle texture I find it hard to beat. This stitch lends elegance to any pattern, but it is also extremely practical: because it doesn't curl up, no added edgings are needed.

To make this scarf, I cast on in a contrasting colour before changing to the main shade to start knitting. I then also made the tassels for the fringing in the contrasting colour, but of course you could make the scarf in a single colour if you prefer. As this is one of my simple 'oblong' patterns, with no shaping, you can easily make your scarf longer or shorter than mine if you like.

YOU WILL NEED

5 × 50 g (1¾ oz) balls of Debbie Bliss Cashmerino Aran in Conker (A); 1 × 50 g (1¾ oz) ball in Charcoal (B)

Pair of 5 mm (US 8) knitting needles

TENSION/GAUGE

Using 5 mm (US 8) needles and working in moss/seed st, 18 sts and 28 rows = 10 cm (4 in) square

FINISHED SIZE

175 × 22 cm (69 × 8½ in), excluding fringe

LEVEL

Moving on

TIP

To make a hoody scarf for a child, look at your tension/gauge and work out the required number of stitches for the width you'd like – about a third fewer stitches should be fine.

METHOD

With 5 mm (US 8) needles and B cast on 40 sts.
Change to A and work in moss/seed st as foll.

Row 1: K1, P1.
Row 2: P1, K1.
Rep Rows 1–2 for 160 cm (63 in). Change to B and cast/
bind off.

To finish

Fold the scarf in half lengthways. From the fold, sew down
one side only for 25 cm (10 in) to form the seam for the
back of the head. Sew in any loose ends.

Fringe

Using B, wrap a strand of yarn 5 times around a book
about 30 cm (12 in) wide (this can vary depending on
how long you want the fringe to be). Cut and remove from
the book, giving 10 strands of yarn the same length. Fold
over and thread the folded end through one end of the
scarf, carefully opening up a hole between sts to pass
the thread through **(a)**. Pass the loose ends through the
folded edge to secure the fringe to the edge of your scarf
(b). Rep to add 8 tassels in total across the end of the
scarf. Rep with another 8 tassels at the other end of
the scarf.

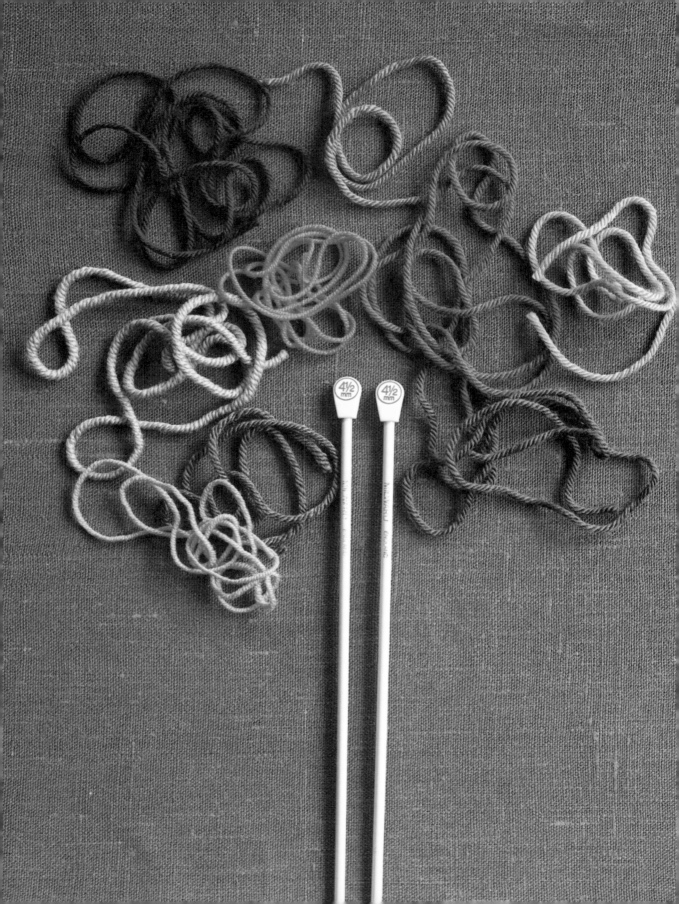

HEADS YOU WIN

Knitted hats are the obvious way to go on cold days: a high percentage of body heat escapes through your head, so keep it covered up! You can look cool while keeping warm with this selection of knitted headgear in a variety of styles, from a basic beanie to a Sherlock-style hat with earflaps. Suitable for girls and boys, women and men, woolly hats are quick and satisfying to knit. Once you've made one for yourself, why not make some more for your partner, friends or children?

EAR HAT

Quirky knitted hats have been popular for a while now, and I've always included a few when designing children's knits for my Little Badger label, from cat hats and dog hats to a red beanie with horns and a tail that makes a cute little devil. I've had many requests for similar styles to fit adults, so this adorable hat with ears (a bear or a cat, depending on your mood) is my response.

This simple design is based on a knitted oblong, which even a novice knitter should be able to whip up in no more than a couple of evenings. The basic chunky rib worked in a soft yarn means you'll get no complaints about comfort or 'scratchy wool'. The colour is neutral, which I think gives this hat a cool, sophisticated feel despite its quirky and fun design. The name of the design notwithstanding, you could ignore the ear shaping altogether and add a pom pom to each corner instead, or leave the hat plain and unadorned for a completely different look.

YOU WILL NEED

2 × 50 g (1¾ oz) balls of Debbie Bliss Rialto Chunky in Sage

Pair of 6.5 mm (US 10½) and pair of 5.5 mm (US 9) knitting needles

Tapestry needle

TENSION/GAUGE

Using 5.5 mm (US 9) needles and working in K2, P2 rib, 14 sts and 21 rows = 10 cm (4 in) square when steam ironed flat

FINISHED SIZE

46 × 19 cm (18 × 7½ in)

LEVEL

Moving on

TIPS

You could make two hats with 3 × 50 g (1¾ oz) balls. To make a larger hat add stitches in groups of four.

METHOD

With 5.5 mm (US 9) needles cast on 64 sts.
Row 1: K2, P2.
Rep Row 1 for 4 rows.
Change to 6.5 mm (US 10½) needles and cont in patt until work measures 19 cm (7½ in). Cast/bind off.

To finish

Fold in half lengthways and stitch along the side seam and top edge with mattress stitch from the RS or backstitch on the WS.

Ear shapes

Beg 14 cm (5½ in) from the bottom edge, sew a diagonal line in a neat running stitch to 6 cm (2½ in) in along the top seam from the side. Rep on the opposite side. These will form 2 triangles, which, when the hat is worn, look like cat's ears.

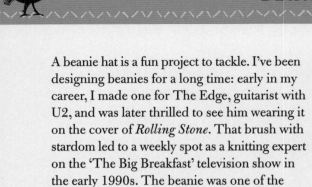

BEANIE HATS

A beanie hat is a fun project to tackle. I've been designing beanies for a long time: early in my career, I made one for The Edge, guitarist with U2, and was later thrilled to see him wearing it on the cover of *Rolling Stone*. That brush with stardom led to a weekly spot as a knitting expert on the 'The Big Breakfast' television show in the early 1990s. The beanie was one of the styles I chose to teach the ebullient presenter Paula Yates to make, and I like to think that I was on trend then and still am today.

I have made three versions of the basic beanie: a plain one for men, a block stripe for women and a jolly stripy style for children. There's nothing to stop you from knitting a stripy men's hat, of course – make these designs your own by changing the colours, the width of stripes or adding a pom-pom to the top. Using the basic shape as a blueprint, you could even knit a beanie using a textured stitch.

VARIATION 1: CHILD'S BEANIE

YOU WILL NEED
1 × 50 g (1¾ oz) ball of Debbie Bliss Rialto 4 ply in Fuchsia (A); 1 × 50 g (1¾ oz) ball in Tangerine (B)

Pair of 3.25 mm (US 3) knitting needles

Tapestry needle

TENSION/GAUGE
Using 3.25 mm (US 3) needles and working in st st, 28 sts and 38 rows = 10 cm (4 in) square

FINISHED SIZE
40 cm (15¾ in) all round × 15 cm (6 in)

LEVEL
Moving on

METHOD
With 3.25 mm (US 3) needles and B cast on 114 sts, using the cable method (see page 17).
Change to A.
Rows 1–4: Knit.
Change to B.
Rows 5–8: Knit.
Change to A.
Rows 9–12: Work in st st.
Change to B and cont in st st, changing colour every 4 rows, until the end of Row 22.
Row 23: K2, K2tog, [K10, K2tog] 9 times, K2. (104 sts)
Row 24: Purl.
Change to A.
Row 25: Knit.
Row 26: Purl.
Row 27: K6, K2tog, [K11, K2tog] 7 times, K5. (96 sts)
Row 28: Purl.

Change to B.
Row 29: Knit.
Row 30: Purl.
Row 31: K1, K2tog, [K14 , K2tog] 5 times, K13. (90 sts)
Row 32: Purl.
Change to A.
Row 33: Knit.
Row 34: Purl.
Row 35: K1, K2tog, [K13, K2tog] 5 times, K12. (84 sts)
Row 36: Purl.
Change to B.
Row 37: K1, K2tog, [K12, K2tog] 5 times, K11. (78 sts)
Row 38: Purl.
Cont dec as set, keeping stripes correct, until Row 57. (18 sts)
Row 58: Purl.
Row 59: [K1, K2tog] 6 times. (12 sts)

To finish

Cut thread to 30 cm (12 in) long. Using a tapestry needle,
thread the end through all 12 sts and pull up tight. Use
the same end to sew the seam in mattress stitch from the
RS or backstitch on the WS. Sew in any loose ends.

VARIATION 2: MAN'S BEANIE

YOU WILL NEED

1 × 50 g (1¾ oz) ball of Debbie Bliss Rialto Aran
in Charcoal (A); 1 × 50 g (1¾ oz) ball in Lime (B)

Pair of 5 mm (US 8) knitting needles

Tapestry needle

TENSION/GAUGE

Using 5 mm (US 8) needles and working in st st,
18 sts and 24 rows = 10 cm (4 in) square

FINISHED SIZE

50 cm (20½ in) all around × 18 cm (7 in)

LEVEL

Moving on

TIP

You can use any leftover yarn as a contrasting edge.
I used an end of Lime yarn to cast on.

METHOD

With 5 mm (US 8) needles and B cast on 90 sts,
using the cable method of casting on (see page 17).
Change to A.

Rows 1–6: Knit.

Row 7 (RS): Knit.

Row 8: Purl.

Cont in st st until the end of Row 22.

Row 23: K1, K2tog, K12, [K2tog, K13] 5 times.
(84 sts)

Row 24: Purl.

Row 25: K1, K2tog, K11, [K2tog, K12] 5 times.
(78 sts)

Row 26: Purl.

Row 27: K1, K2tog, K10, [K2tog, K11] 5 times.
(72 sts)

Row 28: Purl.

Cont dec as set until 18 sts rem.

To finish

Cut thread to about 30 cm (12 in) long. Using
a tapestry needle, thread the end through all 18 sts
and pull up tight. Use the same end to sew the side
seam in mattress stitch from the RS or backstitch
on the WS. Sew in any loose ends securely.

VARIATION 3: WOMAN'S BEANIE

YOU WILL NEED

1 × 50 g (1¾ oz) ball of Debbie Bliss Cashmerino DK in Plum (A); 1 × 50 g (1¾ oz) in Airforce (B)

Pair of 4 mm (US 6) knitting needles

Tapestry needle

TENSION/GAUGE

Using 4 mm (US 6) needles and working in st st, 22 sts and 30 rows = 10 cm (4 in) square

FINISHED SIZE

46 cm (18 in) all around × 15 cm (6 in)

LEVEL

Moving on

METHOD

With 4 mm (US 6) needles and B cast on 102 sts. Change to A.

Rows 1–6: Knit.

Row 7: (RS) Knit.

Row 8: Purl.

Cont in st st until the end of Row 20.

Change to B and cont in st st until the end of Row 22.

Row 23: K1, K2tog, K14, [K2tog, K15] 5 times. (96 sts)

Row 24: Purl.

Row 25: K1, K2tog, K13, [K2tog, K14] 5 times. (90 sts)

Row 26: Purl.

Row 27: K1, K2tog, K12, [K2tog, K13] 5 times. (84 sts)

Row 28: Purl.

Cont dec as set until Row 38. (54 sts)

Row 39: K1, K2tog, K6, [K2tog, K7] 5 times. (48 sts)

Row 40: Purl.

Change to A, leaving an end of B long enough to sew the side seam.

Row 41: K1, K2tog, K5, [K2tog, K6] 5 times. (42 sts)

Row 42: Purl.

Cont dec as set until Row 46. (30 sts)

Row 47: K1, K2tog, K2, [K2tog, K3] 5 times. (24 sts)

To finish

Cut thread to about 30 cm (12 in) long. Using a tapestry needle, thread the end through all 24 sts and pull up tight. Sew the seam in mattress stitch from the RS or backstitch on the WS. Sew in any loose ends securely.

I started collecting old knitting patterns when I was an art student, regularly finding them in thrift shops for pennies. Consequently, I have a huge collection of them and these vintage patterns serve as a source of inspiration for many of my designs.

The beret is one of those fashion items that recurs from decade to decade. I have lots of patterns for knitted hats, including a variety of berets: some are plain, many are in traditional Fair Isle patterns and there are a few Aran hats, too. These patterns are usually far too fussy for today's stylish knitter, particularly the Aran styles, which often use a wide variety of cable stitches on one hat. So I've designed this modern cabled beret with clean lines. Steering well clear of the cream wool of a traditional Aran, it's knitted in a soft, thick yarn in a flattering and fashionable shade.

If you haven't tackled cable knitting before, try a few sample cables before you start the project – I think you'll be surprised by how easy and effective this method is. The twisted 'cable' element is worked every six or eight rows, with the remaining rows made up of stocking/stockinette and reverse stocking/stockinette stitch.

YOU WILL NEED

3 × 50 g (1¾ oz) balls of Debbie Bliss Cashmerino Aran in Teal (used double)

6.5 mm (US 10½) and 4 mm (US 6) circular needles; double-pointed needle (dpn) or cable needle

Tapestry needle

TENSION/GAUGE

Using 6.5 mm (US 10½) needles and working in st st with yarn used double, 14 sts and 20 rows = 10 cm (4 in) square

FINISHED SIZE

28 cm (11 in) across

LEVEL

Going further

TIP

You should use circular needles because of the number of stitches not knitted in the round.

METHOD

With a 4 mm (US 6) circular needle and yarn used double, cast on 77 sts.

Row 1 (RS): [K2, P2] to last st, K1.

Row 2 (WS): P1, [K2, P2] to end.

Rep Rows 1 and 2 twice more.

Row 7: As Row 1.

Row 8 (WS): P1, [K1, M1, K1, P2] to end. (96 sts)

Change to a 6.5 mm (US 10½) circular needle.

Row 1 (RS): P2, K6, [P13, K6] to last 12 sts, P12.

Row 2 (WS): K12, [P6, K13] to last 8 sts, P6, K2.

Row 3: As Row 1.

Row 4: K1, M1, K9, M1, K2, [P6, K2, M1, K9, M1, K2] to last 8 sts, P6, K2. (106 sts)

Row 5 (RS, cable row): P2, *sl next 3 sts on to dpn and hold at the back, K next 3 sts, K3 sts from dpn, P15*, rep from * to *, ending last rep P14 instead of P15.

Row 6 (WS): K14, [P6, K15] to last 8 sts, P6, K2.

Row 7 (RS): P2, [K6, P15] rep ending last rep P14 instead of P15.

Rows 8, 10, 12 and 14: As Row 6.

Rows 9, 11, 13: As Row 7.

Row 15 (RS, cable row): P1, *sl next 4 sts on to dpn and hold at the back, K next 4 sts, (K1, M1, K1, M1, K2 from dpn), P13*, rep from * to * to end.

Note that all WS rows end with a K1.

Row 16 (WS): [K13, P10] to last st, K1.

Rows 17 and 19 (RS): P1, [K10, P13] to end. (116 sts)

Rows 18 and 20 (WS): As Row 16.

Row 21 (RS): P1, K9, ssk, [P11, K2tog, K8, ssk] to last 12 sts, P10, P2tog. (106 sts)

Rows 22 and 24: [K11, P10] to last st, K1.

Row 23: P1, [K10, P11] to end.

Row 25: P1, K9, ssk, [P9, K2tog, K8, ssk] to last 10 sts, P8, P2tog. (96 sts)

Rows 26 and 28: [K9, P10] to last st, K1.

Row 27: P1, [K10, P9] to end.

Row 29 (RS, cable row): P1, *sl 6 sts on to dpn and hold at back, K4, (K2tog, K2tog, K2 from dpn), P9*, rep from * to * to end. (86 sts)

Rows 30 and 32: [K9, P8] to last st, K1.

Row 31: P1, [K8, P9] to end.

Row 33: P1, K7, ssk, [P7, K2tog, K6, ssk] to last 8 sts, P6, P2tog. (76 sts)

Row 34: [K7, P8] to last st, K1.

Row 35 (RS, cable row): P1, *sl 4 sts on to dpn and hold at back, K4 (K2tog, K2tog from dpn), P7*, rep from * to * to end. (66 sts)

Row 36: [K7, P6] to last st, K1.

Row 37 (RS): P1, K5, ssk, [P5, K2tog, K4, ssk] to last 6 sts, P4, P2tog. (56 sts)

Row 38: [K5, P6] to last st, K1.

Row 39: P1, K5, ssk, [P3, K2tog, K4, ssk] to last 4 sts, P2, P2tog. (46 sts)

Row 40: [K3, P6] to last st, K1.

Row 41: P1, [K3tog tbl, K3tog, P3tog] to end. (16 sts)

To finish

Leave an end of 45 cm (17¾ in). With RS facing, thread the yarn through the remaining sts twice and pull up tight. Use the remaining yarn to sew the side seam with mattress stitch from the RS. Sew in any ends.

SHERLOCK POM-POM HAT

Although this hat is not quite a deerstalker, the earflaps do bring to mind London's most famous detective – hence the name. Warm, cute and fashionable to boot, the Sherlock hat is a quick knit. The basic shape is very similar to that of the beanies on page 62, but with the addition of the earflaps knitted in garter stitch and the pom-poms, the finished item looks quite different.

The pom-poms and the twisted wool cord they hang from are easy and fun to make. Pom-poms are a wonderful finishing touch to many projects and work particularly well on this design, but if you prefer something less fussy just leave them off – the hat will keep your ears just as warm. You will need to pick up stitches for the earflaps, but that part is not terribly tricky: you can follow the instructions in steps 3 and 4 of shaping the heel of a sock on page 27. As with the beanies, you could try knitting a striped version of this hat, or you could knit the garter stitch bands and earflaps in a second colour.

YOU WILL NEED

3 × 50 g (1¾ oz) balls of Debbie Bliss Cashmerino Aran in Mulberry; if you prefer to make smaller pom-poms use 2 × 50 g (1¾ oz) balls

Pair of 5 mm (US 8) knitting needles

Tapestry needle

TENSION/GAUGE

Using 5 mm (US 8) and working in st st, 18 sts and 24 rows = 10 cm (4 in) square

FINISHED SIZE

Circumference (unstretched) 50.5 cm (20 in); depth from crown to edge of hat 20 cm (8 in); flaps 10 × 7.5 cm (4 × 3 in), excluding cords and pom-poms

LEVEL

Moving on

METHOD

With 5 mm (US 8) needles cast on 91 sts, using the cable method of casting on (see page 17).

Rows 1–8: Knit.
Row 9 (RS): Knit.
Row 10: Purl.
Cont in st st until the end of Row 30.
Row 31: K1, K2tog, K13, [K2tog, K13] 5 times. (85 sts)
Row 32: Purl.
Row 33: K1, K2tog, K12, [K2tog, K12] 5 times. (79 sts)
Row 34: Purl.
Row 35: K1, K2tog, K11, [K2tog, K11] 5 times. (73 sts)
Cont dec in this way until 25 sts rem.
Last row: P1, then P2tog across row. (13 sts)
Cut thread to about 30 cm (12 in) long. Using a tapestry needle, thread the end through all 13 sts twice and pull up tight. Use the same end to sew the side seam in mattress stitch from the RS or backstitch from the WS.

Right ear flap

With RS facing and starting on the 14th st from the edge, pick up 19 sts along the cast-on edge.
Work 11 rows in garter st.
Row 12: K2, K2tog, K11, K2tog, K2. (17 sts)
Row 13: Knit.
Row 14: K2, K2tog, K9, K2tog, K2. (15 sts)
Row 15: Knit.
Row 16: K2, K2tog, K7, K2tog, K2. (13 sts)
Row 17: Knit.
Row 18: K2, K2tog, K5, K2tog, K2. (11 sts)
Row 19: K2, K2tog, K3, K2tog, K2. (9 sts)
Row 20: K2, K2tog, K1, K2tog, K2. (7 sts)
Row 21: K1, K2tog, K1, K2tog, K1. (5 sts)
Row 22: K2tog, K1, K2tog. (3 sts)
Cast/bind off. Sew in any loose ends securely. With RS facing and starting on the 32nd st from the edge rep on the opposite side for the left ear flap. Sew the back seam.

Pom-poms

Make 3 pom-poms.
a. Cut two circles of card, each about 8 cm (3¼ in) in diameter. Cut a smaller hole in the centre of each circle, about half the size of the original diameter. The larger this hole, the fuller the pom-pom will be. Holding the two card rings together, wind the yarn around them (you can use several strands at a time for speed) until the ring is completely covered. As the hole at the centre gets smaller, you may find it easier to use a tapestry needle to pass the yarn through.
b. Using a pair of sharp scissors, cut through all the wrapped yarn around the outside edge between the two circles. Make sure all the yarn has been cut.
c. Separate the two circles slightly. Join in a length of yarn by wrapping the two tails from one end in opposite directions around the centre of the pom-pom and secure firmly with a knot, leaving a long end – you will use this to sew the pom-poms to the top of the hat and to the cords.
d. Pull the two circles apart and fluff out the pom-pom to cover the centre join. Trim the pom-pom if necessary.

Twisted cord

Make 2 twisted cords, each approximately 11 cm (4¼ in) long.
Cut three 30cm (12 in) lengths of yarn and knot the strands together at each end. Attach one end to a hook or door handle and insert a knitting needle through the other end. Twist the needle: the tighter the twisting, the firmer the finished cord will be.
Hold the cord in the centre with one hand (you may need some help) and then bring the ends of the cord together. Take care to keep the cord straight and avoid tangling. Knot the cut ends together and trim.

To finish

Attach the twisted cords to the ear flaps. Sew the pom-poms to the top of the hat and to the cords.

While this ever so simple project may seem to be very 'of the moment', this is a tremendously useful piece of knitting: both stylish and practical, a wide knitted band will keep your ears warm and your hair off your face at any time of year.

The plain version is easy enough for the beginner knitter to make in an evening. The slightly more complex cable style may take a few hours more, but it's worth the effort, as it combines the trend for plaited 'up do' hairstyles with the crafter's desire to knit something a little special. I made these ear warmers in natural colours – you can pick a shade that matches your hair – but once you have made your first headband you could quickly make a second in a bright colour. And then a third or a fourth, either for yourself or as a homemade gift that makes a fashion statement.

VARIATION 1: PLAIN EAR WARMER

YOU WILL NEED

1 × 50 g (1¾ oz) ball of Debbie Bliss Cashmerino Aran in Bark

Pair of 5 mm (US 8) knitting needles

TENSION/GAUGE

Using 5 mm (US 8) needles and working in st st, 18 sts and 24 rows = 10 cm (4 in) square

FINISHED SIZE

48 × 8 cm (19 × 3¼ in)

LEVEL

Starting out

METHOD

With 5 mm (US 8) needles cast on 94 sts.
Work in K2, P2 rib for 10 rows as foll:
Row 1: K2, P2.
Row 2: P2, K2.
Rep Rows 1–2 three times more. (8 rows)
Row 9: Knit.
Row 10: Purl.
Rep Rows 9–10 three times more
Rep Rows 1–2 four times more.
Cast/bind off.

To finish

Sew the side seam with neat backstitch from the WS.
Sew in any loose ends.

VARIATION 2: PLAITED CABLE EAR WARMER

YOU WILL NEED

1 × 50 g (1¾ oz) ball of Debbie Bliss Cashmerino Aran in Bark

Pair of 4.5 mm (US 7) knitting needles; double-pointed needle (dpn) or cable needle

TENSION/GAUGE

9-st cable panel measures 4 cm (1½ in) wide

FINISHED SIZE

48 × 8 cm (19 × 3¼ in); 48 cm (19 in) comfortably stretches to fit an average head size of 56–58 cm (22–23 in), but if you need to add length continue in pattern until you reach the required length before casting/binding off

LEVEL

Going further

TIP

Knitting on smaller needles than are recommended on the yarn ball band will give a good, tight tension/gauge.

METHOD

With 4.5 mm (US 7) needles cast on 21 sts.

Row 1 (RS): K4, P2, K9, P2, K4.

Row 2: K6, P9, K6.

Row 3: K4, P2, sl next 3 sts on to dpn and hold in front, K3, then K3 from dpn, K3, P2, K4.

Rows 4 and 6: As Row 2.

Row 5: As Row 1.

Row 7: K4, P2, K3, sl next 3 sts on to dpn and hold at back , K3, then K3 from dpn, P2, K4.

Row 8: As Row 2.

Rep in patt until work measures 48 cm (19 in), finishing on a patt Row 1 or Row 5.

Cast/bind off and sew cast-on edge to cast/bound-off edge with mattress stitch from the RS or backstitch from the WS.

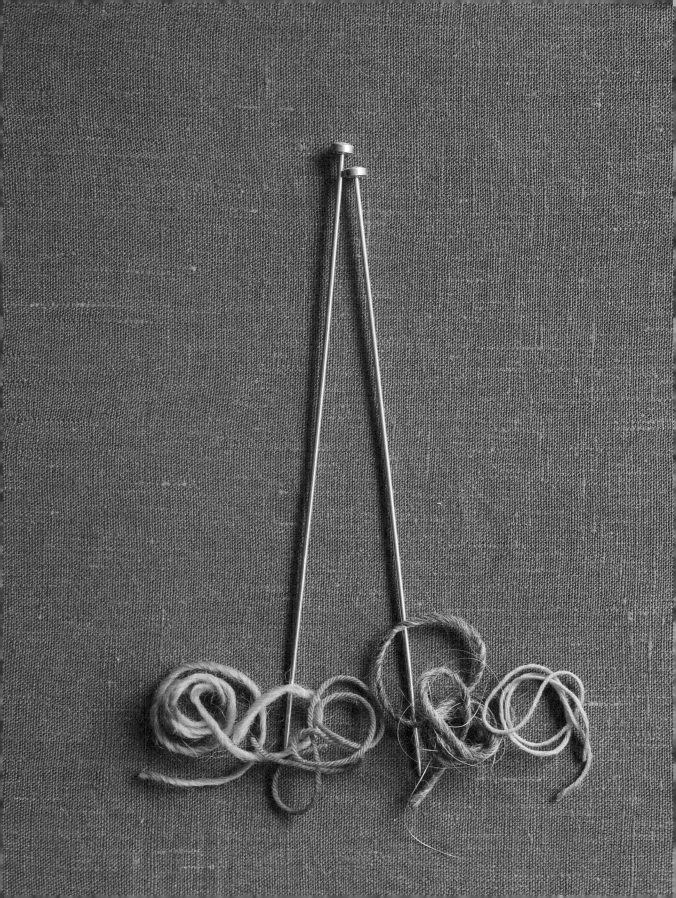

FINGERS AND TOES

With a pair of toasty mittens and some summery cotton
fingerless gloves, you've got all seasons covered. A pair
of wrist warmers is a necessity if, like many of us, you're
tied to your mobile phone, music player or e-reader at all
times, even when out and about, which means cold hands
in winter. Quick and easy to knit, wrist warmers will keep
your fingers warm while also allowing you to answer your
smartphone and press those tiny buttons.

Instead of slippers, I often pad about the house in a pair of
slouchy socks, just like one of the designs in this chapter
– soft and warm, they can double up as bed socks, too.
The sparkly ankle socks, however, are designed to be seen,
absolutely on trend with girls from Inverness to Ipswich,
who love to pair their high heels with short socks.

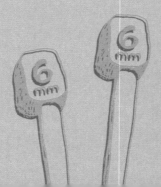

SLOUCHY SOCKS

Even experienced knitters may find the idea of making their first pair of socks daunting, but once you have tried this simple pattern, you will soon find yourself knitting as many pairs as time allows. The traditional way of making socks is to knit them in the round, using a set of five double-pointed needles. To keep things simple for beginners, I have written a pattern using only two needles, with a flat seam running up the back of the sock. Even a relative novice should be able to produce a desirable, wearable pair of socks in next to no time. Knitted in a wool and alpaca yarn, these socks will keep your feet wonderfully warm, whether you wear them in bed or with a pair of wellington boots. You could even sew a piece of leather to the sole and wear them as slippers. Either way, it won't be long before your friends will be knocking at your door, begging you to rustle up a pair for them, too.

In this pattern, the top of the rib and the toe are knitted in a contrasting colour, but there are endless possibilities: knitting stripes, working the whole rib in a contrast colour or knitting the heel in the same colour as the rib and toe.

YOU WILL NEED

1 × 100 g (3½ oz) ball each of Rowan Creative Focus Worsted in Charcoal Heather (A) and New Fern (B)

Pair of 4.5 mm (US 7) knitting needles

Tapestry needle

TENSION/GAUGE

Using 4.5 mm (US 7) needles and working in st st, 20 sts and 24 rows = 10 cm (4 in) square

FINISHED SIZE

To fit UK 4–7 (EU 37–40; US 6.5–9.5)

LEVEL

Going further

TIPS

So that the seam is flat when each sock is sewn up, knit the first and last stitch at the end of every purl row and purl the first and last stitch at the end of every knit row.

This pair of socks weighs about 125 g (4 oz), so three balls would make two pairs of socks, bearing in mind that you need about 25 g (1 oz) of the contrasting colour.

METHOD

Make two.

With 4.5 mm (US 7) needles and A cast on 48 sts.

Change to B, leaving an end of about 30 cm (12 in).

Work in K2, P2 rib as foll:

Row 1: P1, [K2, P2] to last 3 sts, K2, P1.

Row 2: K1, [P2, K2] to last 3 sts, P2, K1.

Rep Rows 1–2 seven times more. (16 rows in B)

Change to A, leaving an end of about 100 cm (40 in).

Work Rows 1–2 four times more. (8 rows in A)

Cont in st st for 41 rows, ending with WS facing.

Work should measure 27 cm (10½ in).

Shape heel

Row 1: K1, P11, turn.

Row 2: Sl1, K to last st, P1.

Row 3: K1, P10, turn.

Row 4: Sl1, K to last st, P1.

Row 5: K1, P9, turn.

Row 6: Sl1, K to last st, P1.

Row 7: K1, P8, turn.

Row 8: Sl1, K to last st, P1.

Row 9: K1, P7, turn.

Row 10: Sl1, K to last st, P1.

Row 11: K1, P6, turn.

Row 12: Sl1, K to last st, P1.

Row 13: K1, P5, turn.

Row 14: Sl1, K to last st, P1.

Next 15: K1, P6, turn.

Row 16: Sl1, K to last st, P1.

Cont in patt as set until the end of RS row sl1, K10, P1.

Next row: K1, P10, P2tog, P to last st, K1. (This row is across all sts.)

Half the heel is now complete. Cont on the second half.

Row 1 (RS): P1, K11, turn.

Row 2: Sl1, P to last st, K1.

Row 3: P1, K10, turn.

Cont in patt as set until the end of WS row sl1, P10, K1.

Next row (RS): P1, K10, ssk, K to last st, P1. (This row is across all sts.)

This is the end of the heel. You should now be back to 46 sts. Starting on WS, work 23 rows in st st. Cont reversing the first and last stitch. End on a WS row.

Shape toe

Change to B.

Row 1: P1, K to last st, P1.

Row 2: K1, P to last st, K1.

Row 3: P1, K6, K2tog, [K7, K2tog] 4 times, P1.

Row 4 and all foll WS rows: K1, P to last st, K1.

Row 5: P1, K5, K2tog, [K6, K2tog] 4 times, P1.

Row 7: P1, K4, K2tog, [K5, K2tog] 4 times, P1.

Cont as set until the end of RS row P1, K2tog, [K1, K2tog] 4 times, P1. (11 sts)

To finish

Transfer 11 sts to the opposite needle and cut the yarn, leaving about 20 cm (8 in). Thread this through a blunt tapestry needle, thread through the 11 sts and draw together gently.

Sew the seam of the sock together with mattress stitch from the RS. A single thread is fine for the rib section, but using a double thread for the st st will add strength. Pick up one loop from each side and pull together gently to make as flat and even a seam as possible.

Use a steam iron or a damp cloth to press the socks into shape.

When I was a party girl in my twenties, it was fashionable to wear ankle socks, often fluorescent in colour, over tights or with leggings. The fashionistas of today are also wearing ankle socks but in a much cooler way than I did: they wear them over sparkly tights and with high heels. These party socks are my contribution to that style. They have been approved by my teenage daughters – high praise indeed – and I think they look great worn here with a pair of gorgeous vintage shoes.

I knitted a silver filament thread in with the 4-ply (fingering) sock yarn, as I wanted to give these ankle socks a contemporary feel and happened to have a reel of silver thread to hand. I later found a gorgeous hand-dyed yarn that I want to use for the next pair I make. Next time I'll make them a mid-calf length by knitting up to 20 cm (8 in) instead of 15 cm (6 in) before shaping the instep.

YOU WILL NEED

2 × 50 g (1¾ oz) balls of 4-ply sock yarn

Pair of 3.25 mm (US 3) and pair of 3.75 mm (US 5) knitting needles

2 × stitch holders

TENSION/GAUGE

Using 3.75 mm (US 5) needles and working in st st, 25 sts and 34 rows = 10 cm (4 in) square

FINISHED SIZE

Length of foot 23.5 cm (9¼ in)

LEVEL

Going further

TIP

I also used a silver filament thread to add sparkle, but this is optional and won't change the tension/gauge.

METHOD

Make two.

With 3.25 mm (US 3) needles cast on 49 sts.

Work in K1, P1 rib for 8 rows; note that alt rows start with P1.

Change to 3.75 mm (US 5) needles and beg patt as foll:

Row 1 (RS facing): P2, [K3, P3] to last 5 sts, K3, P2.

Row 2: K2, [P3, K3] to last 5 sts, P3, K2.

Row 3: P2, [sl1, yo, K2tog, psso, yrn, P3] to last 5 sts, sl1, yo, K2tog, psso, yrn, P2.

Row 4: As Row 2.

Rep rows 1–4 until work measures 15 cm (6 in). (You can adjust the length here for a longer sock or finish before 15 cm (6 in) for a shorter sock, but always finish on Row 4 of the patt.)

Ending on Row 4 of patt, divide sts for instep as foll:

Row 1: (RS facing) P2, [K3, P3] to last 12 sts. Keep these sts on a stitch holder. Turn.

Row 2: K2, [P3, K3] to last 12 sts. Keep these sts on a second stitch holder. (25 sts)

Cont in patt for a further 15 cm (6 in), ending on a Row 4. Working in st st, start toe shaping as foll.

**Next row: K1, K2tog, K to last 3 sts, K2tog, K1. (23 sts)

Next row: Purl.

Rep the last 2 rows until 13 sts rem. Work 1 row. Cast/bind off.

Sew the centre back seam with mattress stitch from the RS.

With RS facing, slip the two lots of 12 heel sts on to one needle from left to right and knit across, increasing 1 st at the centre. (25 sts)

Work the heel

Work 15 further rows in st st, ending on a P row.

Row 1: K15, K2tog, turn.

Row 2: Sl1 purlwise, P5, P2tog, turn.

Rep Row 2, knitting instead of purling on the RS rows, until 7 sts rem.

Next row: K7, pick up 9 sts along the side of the heel,

miss first row then pick up every second and third rows, missing last row (see page 27). (9 sts)

Next row: P16, pick up 9 sts along other side of the heel. Work these 25 sts in st st until they measure the same length as the instep up to the toe shaping, ending with a P row.

Then shape toe shaping as on the instep from **.

Join the two instep seams and the toe seam.

Variation

Instead of casting/binding off the toe stitches you can keep them on a stitch holder, then steam iron flat and graft the instep and sole toe stitches together to avoid a seam. I don't include details in this book, but the instructions are widely available online if you want to try this method.

WRIST WARMERS

Recently, my daughter Martha's friend Claudia – one of an endless stream of cool teenage girls that travel through our house these days – had a sudden desire to learn how to knit. My lovely daughter volunteered my services. Claud, being a typical teenager, was desperate to produce something she could wear straight away but had never picked up a pair of knitting needles before, so I was challenged to come up with a pattern that would keep her keen from the very beginning.

So here it is, the 'no excuse in getting started' glove pattern. The easiest gloves to knit are the fingerless kind, but as the beginner may find increasing for the thumb a little taxing, I designed the simplest of wrist warmers instead: by sewing up one seam, an oblong piece of knitting is transformed into a must-have fashion item. Thick yarn means your work will grow fast, satisfying the most impatient knitter. I finished off the ends with garter stitch, but if you are an absolute beginner you could knit the whole piece in garter stitch, so you wouldn't need to purl at all.

VARIATION 1: ARAN WRIST WARMERS

YOU WILL NEED

1 × 50 g (1¾ oz) ball of Debbie Bliss Rialto Aran in Lime (A) and small amount of Charcoal Grey (B)

....

Pair of 5 mm (US 8) knitting needles

TENSION/GAUGE

Using 5 mm (US 8) needles and working in st st, 18 sts and 24 rows = 10 cm (4 in) square

FINISHED SIZE

8.5 cm (3½ in) flat; 17 cm (6½ in) all around × 18 cm (7 in) finished length

LEVEL

Starting out

METHOD

Make two.
With 5mm (US 8) needles and B, cast on 30 sts using the cable method (see page17).
Change to A and work 6 rows in garter st.
Row 7 (RS): Knit.
Row 8: Purl.
Cont in st st until the end of Row 40.
Rows 41–45: Knit.
Row 46: Cast/bind off knitwise.

To finish

Sew the side seam 7 cm (2¾ in) from the top and 6 cm (2½ in) from the bottom edge, leaving a 5 cm (2 in) gap in the middle for the thumb hole. Secure all ends.

YOU WILL NEED

1 × 50 g (1¾ oz) ball of Debbie Bliss Rialto Chunky in Lilac

Pair of 6.5 mm (US 10½) knitting needles

TENSION/GAUGE

Using 6.5 mm (US 10½) needles and working in st st, 14 sts and 21 rows = 10 cm (4 in) square

FINISHED SIZE

8.5 cm (3½ in); 17 cm (6½ in) all around × 19 cm (7½ in) finished length

LEVEL

Starting out

METHOD

Make two.

With 6.5 mm (US 10½) needles cast on 24 sts using the cable method (see page 17).

Work 6 rows in garter st (knit every row).

Row 7 (RS): Knit.

Row 8: Purl.

Cont in st st until the end of Row 38.

Rows 39–43: Knit.

Cast/bind off knitwise.

To finish

Sew the side seam 7.5 cm (3 in) from the top and 7.5 cm (3 in) from the bottom edge, leaving a 4 cm (1½ in) gap in the middle for the thumb hole.

Secure all ends.

There was a time when a proper lady would wear gloves all year round, wool in winter and cotton in summer, to protect her delicate skin. Those times are long gone, and we consider ourselves lucky if we remember to use hand cream every day. Instead, the trend today is for fingerless gloves, which are very practical as well as fashionable: I find my fingerless gloves extremely useful when driving or when searching for change in my purse. Many people prefer wearing cotton to wool all year round, so this pretty pair of gloves would work with almost any outfit.

These gloves are slightly more complicated to make than the wrist warmers on pages 90 and 92, as they involve some shaping and the addition of a thumb. This is therefore a great little project on which to practise how to increase stitches, an essential part of your knitting knowledge. The same goes for working a picot edge and making decorative little holes, also known as pointelle – both very useful skills to have. Of course you could make the gloves without the picot edge and the little holes by ignoring that part of the pattern: feel free to do so if it seems overwhelming, but I think you will find that this technique is a breeze.

YOU WILL NEED

1 × 50 g (1¾ oz) ball of Debbie Bliss Eco Baby in Duck Egg

Pair of 4 mm (US 6) knitting needles

2 × 50 cm lengths of 1 cm (½ in) ribbon; I used a vintage grosgrain ribbon

TENSION/GAUGE

Using 4 mm (US 6) needles and working in st st, 20 sts and 28 rows = 10 cm (4 in) square

FINISHED SIZE

19 × 8 cm (7½ × 3¼ in); 16 cm (6½ in) all around

LEVEL

Going further

METHOD

Make two.

With 4 mm (US 6) needles cast on 35 sts, leaving a
30 cm (12 in) end for joining up later.

Row 1: Knit.

Row 2: Purl.

Row 3: Knit.

Row 4 (WS): P1, [yo, P2tog], to end.

Rows 5 and 7: Knit.

Row 6: Purl.

Row 8 (WS): Insert needle purlwise into first st, pick up
first 'cast-on' loop from cast-on edge and P together.
Cont in same way to end. This forms the picot edge.
(35 sts)

Rows 9 and 11: Knit.

Rows 10 and 12: Purl.

Row 13 (RS): K1, [yf, K2tog, yf, K2tog, K1] to last 4 sts,
yf, K2tog, yf, K2tog **(a)**.

Row 14 (WS): Purl **(b)**. This forms the eyelet row.
Work in st st until work measures 9 cm (3½ in) from picot
edge, ending on a P row.

Inc for thumb.

Next row (RS): K16, M1, K3, M1, K16. (37 sts)

Next row: Purl.

Next row: K16, M1, K5, M1, K16. (39 sts)

Next row: Purl.

Cont inc as set twice more. (43 sts)

Next row (WS): P27, transfer the foll 16 sts to a spare
piece of yarn (not a stitch holder because it needs to be
flexible).

Turn to RS and cast on 2 sts as tightly as possible. Knit
these 2 sts and 11 more (13 sts) and transfer the rem 16
sts to another piece of yarn.

Work the thumb.

Work 5 rows in st st over the 13 sts, beg with a P row,
then, with RS facing, cast/bind off, not too tightly, leaving
a 15 cm (6 in) end. Sew the thumb seam, leaving the end
of yarn loose for later.

With WS facing and starting from the RHS, transfer
the 16 sts from the second length of yarn on to a

needle. With new yarn and leaving a 10 cm (4 in) tail,
pick up purlwise 3 sts from the base of thumb, collect
the remaining 16 sts (held on yarn) on the needle, then,
starting from the left, cont in P until the end of the row.
(35 sts)

With RS facing, K across 1 row, taking care not to
dislodge the 3 'cast-on' sts, then tighten up the picked-up
sts. If necessary, sew another st in the thumb seam. Tie
the loose ends firmly together to be sewn in later.

Cont in st st until work measures 18 cm (7 in) from the
picot edge, ending on a RS row.

Next row (WS): As Row 4.

Work 4 rows more in st st.

Cast/bind off. Cut yarn, leaving an end of about 35 cm
(13¾ in), and sew cast-off (bound-off) edge firmly, stitch
for stitch, to the fifth row before the holes and not quite
to the end.

To finish

Turn the thumb inside out and finish off any loose ends.
Sew the side seam, starting at the cuff edge, up and
over the picot edge, then sew inner side seam. When
completed, sew the thread into the seam to secure, finish
off the cast-off (bound-off) join and sew in that thread
too. Thread ribbon through holes to tie at side edge.

POM-POM MITTENS

One of my favourite childhood memories is of watching snowflakes melting on the tips of my mittens. I am glad to say that mittens have never not been in fashion, so I can confidently predict that you will love making and wearing this cosy pair. The long rib cuff means that you can tuck them up inside your coat sleeves for extra warmth on freezing cold days, or alternatively you can wear the cuff turned down – both options look equally stylish. The pom-poms are purely for fun, with no purpose other than looking pretty, so they are an optional extra.

I like the combination of lilac and stormy grey – these colours remind me of cosy walks by the sea, but maybe I am letting my imagination get carried away with me. If you prefer, you could knit these mittens in a single colour instead of stripes. As with other patterns, using a finer yarn will make a smaller pair, so try a DK (sport weight) or 4-ply (fingering) yarn and create some mittens for children – you could even a make a matching beanie (see page 62). If you're a real retro enthusiast, you could also join the mittens with a long cord and thread it through your coat sleeves, thus guaranteeing that they will never get lost.

YOU WILL NEED

2 × 50 g (1¾ oz) balls of Debbie Bliss Rialto Chunky in Lilac (A); 1 × 50 g (1¾ oz) ball in Storm (B)

Pair of 5 mm (US 8) knitting needles

Tapestry needle

TENSION/GAUGE

Using 5 mm (US 8) needles and working in st st, 16 sts and 23 rows = 10 cm (4 in) square

FINISHED SIZE

Mitten length 32 cm (before rib is folded) width 10 cm (4 in) (20 cm (8 in) all around)

LEVEL

Moving on

METHOD

Make two.

With 5 mm (US 8) needles and A cast on 33 sts.

Work in K1, P1 rib for 23 rows.

Starting with a K row, work 8 rows in st st.

Change to B, leaving enough of an end to sew up the stripe.

Work 2 rows in st st.

Beg inc for thumb.

RS: K15, M1, K3, M1, K to end. (35 sts)

WS: Purl.

Work 2 more rows in st st.

RS: K15, M1, K5, M1, K15. (37 sts)

WS: Purl.

Work 2 more rows in st st.

RS: K15, M1, K7, M1, K15. (39 sts)

WS: P24, turn, sl rem 15 sts on to a fairly long piece of cotton yarn (this is more flexible than a stitch holder).

RS: Cast on 2 sts, then K them with the next 9 sts (11 sts for thumb). Sl the remaining 15 sts on to the cotton thread.

WS: P11.

RS: Change to A and work 10 rows in st st.

Beg dec for thumb.

RS: K2tog 5 times (as tightly as possible), K1. (6 sts)

Cut the yarn, leaving a long enough end to thread through the 6 sts and to sew the seam of the thumb.

Transfer the 6 sts to the opposite needle and thread the yarn through the 6 sts with a tapestry needle. Draw up into a tight circle and thread the yarn through again. Sew the side seam, using B for the last 2 rows in B. Don't cut the yarn yet.

Collect the sts from the cotton yarn on to needles, from outside in, so that the needle points meet at the thumb base.

WS: Leaving a few cm (in) of B, using RH needle pick up purlwise 3 sts at the base of thumb and cont in P to the end of the row. (33 sts)

Work 2 more rows in st st.

RS: Change to A and work 14 rows in st st.

RS: Change to B and work 2 rows in st st.

Dec for finger shaping.

Row 1 (RS): K5, K2tog, [K6, K2tog] to last 2 sts, K2. (29 sts)

Work 3 rows in st st.

Row 5 (RS): K4 , K2tog, [K5, K2tog] to last 2 sts, K2. (25 sts)

Row 6: Purl.

Row 7: K3, K2tog, [K4, K2tog] to last 2 sts, K2. (21 sts)

Row 8: Purl.

Row 9: K2, K2tog, [K3, K2tog] to last 2 sts, K2. (17 sts)

Row 10: [P2, P2tog] to last st, P1. (13 sts)

Cut yarn, leaving an end long enough to sew the seam. Use a tapestry needle to thread the yarn through the remaining sts and draw them up into a tight circle. Thread it through again and sew the side seam with mattress stitch from the RS.

Pom-poms

Make 4 × 4 cm (1½ in) pom-poms, 2 in A, 2 in B (see pages 74–5). When finishing off the pom-poms leave 2 × 10 cm (4 in) lengths of yarn. Thread this through the side seams at the point where the rib finishes, then attach a second pom-pom in same way. Tie all 4 ends together on inside of the mittens and secure firmly by sewing into the side seams.

MARY JANE SLIPPERS

My daughters' first real shoes were Mary Janes, with a single bar and a button fastening. I was so obsessed with these classic children's shoes that I tracked down a version that went up to a UK size 5 so that Martha and Ceidra could continue wearing them well into secondary school. Luckily for me, the Mary Janes appealed to my girls' taste for vintage clothes.

My collection of old knitting patterns includes a few for slippers, so with these homemade shoes in mind, I searched the internet for knitted Mary Janes. There are a number of variations on this theme out there, and I have designed my own to add to them. The rib upper makes a neat shape with a retro feel, but the bright colour and contrast strap move these slippers firmly into the twenty-first century. When I asked my eldest daughter to try them on she didn't want to take them off – always a good sign.

This is a quirky pattern, but if you follow it exactly as it is written everything will become clear as you knit. This project probably sounds a little daunting (and I have to admit that knitting the border is a bit tedious) but the finished slippers are well worth the effort.

 YOU WILL NEED

60 g (2½ oz) Yeoman Yarns Soft Cotton DK in Tango (A) and small amount of Charcoal (B)

4 × 3.75 mm (US 5) double-pointed needles (dpn); 3.25mm (US 3) circular needle; 3.75mm (US 5) circular needle (optional)

2 × small vintage buttons

 TENSION/GAUGE

Using 3.75 mm (US 5) needles and working in garter st, 18 sts and 38 rows = 10 cm (4 in) square

 FINISHED SIZE

About 20 × 11 cm (8 × 4 in), before stretching; UK size 4–6 (EU 37–39; US 6.5–8.5)

 LEVEL

Going further

 TIPS

I used cotton DK yarn from a cone, but if you are using balls you should buy 2 × 50 g (1¾ oz) balls.

Note that ssk is not exactly the same as K2tog tbl; ssk looks exactly like K2tog in reverse, whereas with K2tog tbl the stitches are twisted.

 METHOD

Make two.

Sole

With a pair of 3.75 mm (US 5) dpns and A cast on 6 sts. Beg at the toe end.

Row 1 (RS): Knit.

Note that from now on you should start all rows with slip 1.

Row 2: Sl1, K1, inc 1 (by picking up the loop before the next st and knitting into it), K to last 2 sts, inc 1, K2. (8 sts)

Row 3 and 4: Knit.

Row 5: Sl1, K1, inc 1 (by picking up the loop before the next st and knitting into it), K to last 2 sts, inc 1, K2. (10sts)

Rep Rows 3–5 three times more (16 sts, 8 ridges)

Garter st rows are not easy to count, so count the ridges that appear on the RS of work (note that you count the 'cast on' ridge). The exact number of rows is important.

Rows 15–29: Knit.

Row 30: Sl1, K1, K2tog, K to last 4 sts, ssk, K2. (14 sts, 16 ridges)

Row 31-39: Knit.

Row 40: Sl1, K1, K2tog, K to last 4 sts, ssk, K2. (12 sts, 21 ridges)

Rows 41–67: Knit.

Row 68: Sl1, K1, K2tog, K to last 4 sts, ssk, K2. (10 sts, 35 ridges)

Rows 69 and 70: Knit.

Row 71: Sl1, K1, K2tog, K to last 4 sts, ssk, K2. (8 sts, 36 ridges)

Row 72: Knit.

Row 73: Sl1, K1, K2tog, K to last 4 sts, ssk, K2. (6 sts)

Row 74: Knit. (38 ridges)

Do not cast/bind off.

Sides

Place a marker at the centre of the 6 cast-on sts (see page 35). With the last 6 sts still on the needle, start picking up sts along the side of the sole, 1st in each gap between ridges. When you reach 34 sts (this includes 6 sts from Row 74), start using a 2nd dpn. Pick up stitches in 9 more gaps (the last one may be a bit difficult, but the gap is there). Then pick up 2 of the cast-on sts before the marker and 2 more after the marker, then a further 11 sts between the gaps down the other side. (24 sts on needle)

Start using a 3rd dpn and pick up remaining 26 sts. Note that by the time you get to 3 cm (1¼ in) from the end, it may be too difficult to pick up between the last ridge. If so, slip the first 2 sts (no more) from the beginning of the first dpn onto the 4th dpn. When you have picked up between all the ridges with your 3rd dpn, K the 2 sts from 4th dpn back onto the 3rd dpn.

You now have 32 sts on the 1st needle, 24 sts on the 2nd needle and 28 sts on the 3rd needle. (84 sts total)

Place a marker to mark the beginning of each round.

Round 1: Purl.

Round 2: Knit.

Round 3: Purl.

Change to a 3.75 mm (US 5) circular needle if you prefer and continue.

Round 4: K2, P2 for 32 sts. Add a 2nd marker to remind you where the toe shaping begins. K1, ssk, P2, K2, P3, K2, P3, K2, P2, K2tog, K1, place a 3rd marker to show where the shaping ends, P2, K2 over following 30 sts to the end of the round. (82 sts)

Round 5: K2, P2 to 2nd marker (32 sts), K2, P2, K2, P3, K2, P3, K2, P2, K2 to 3rd marker, then P2, K2 (30 sts) to end of the round. (82 sts)

Round 6: K2, P2 to 2nd marker (32 sts), K2, P2, K1, ssk, P2, K2, P2, K2tog, K1, P2, K2, (3rd marker) then P2, K2 to end. (80 sts)

Round 7: K2, P2 to end. (80 sts)

Round 8: K2, P2 to 2nd marker (32 sts) K1, ssk, P1, K2, P2, K2, P2, K2, P1, K2tog, K1, (3rd marker) then P2, K2 to end. (78 sts)

Round 9: K2, P2 to 2nd marker (32 sts) K2, P1, K2, P2, K2, P2, K2, P1, K2, (3rd marker) then P2, K2 to end. (78sts)

Round 10: K2, P2 to 2nd marker (32 sts), K2, P1, K1, ssk, P1, K2, P1, K2tog, K1, P1, K2 (3rd marker), then P2, K2 to end. (76 sts)

Round 11: K2, P2 to 2nd marker (32 sts), K2, P1, K2, P1, K2, P1, K2, P1, K2 (3rd marker), then P2, K2 to end. (76 sts)

Round 12: K2, P2 to 2nd marker (32 sts), K1, ssk, K1, ssk, K2, K2tog, K1, K2tog, K1 (3rd marker), then P2, K2 to end. (72 sts)

Cast/bind off loosely.

Border

With RS facing, using a 3.25mm (US 3) circular needle and B, pick up all cast/bound-off stitches (complete through both loops). When you are back at the beginning, cast on 2 sts.

Work as foll: *K2, K2tog through the back of the loops, slip these 3 sts back on to the LH needle*; rep from * to * all the way round to form the border. When you have completed the round, either graft the last 3 sts to the first 3, or cast/bind off and neatly sew the cast/bound-off edge to the first 3 sts.

Bar

With B, cast on 2sts, leaving a long end for the button.

Row 1: Knit.

Row 2: K1, inc 1, K1. (3 sts)

Row 3: Knit.

Continue in garter st until the bar measures 10 cm (4 in). Cast/bind off, leaving enough yarn to sew onto the inside edge of slippers, approx 7 cm (2¾ in) from centre back edge. Then using the button to secure, sew the cast-on end of the bar to the outside edge of slippers, overlapping the top edge slightly. Sew in any loose ends.

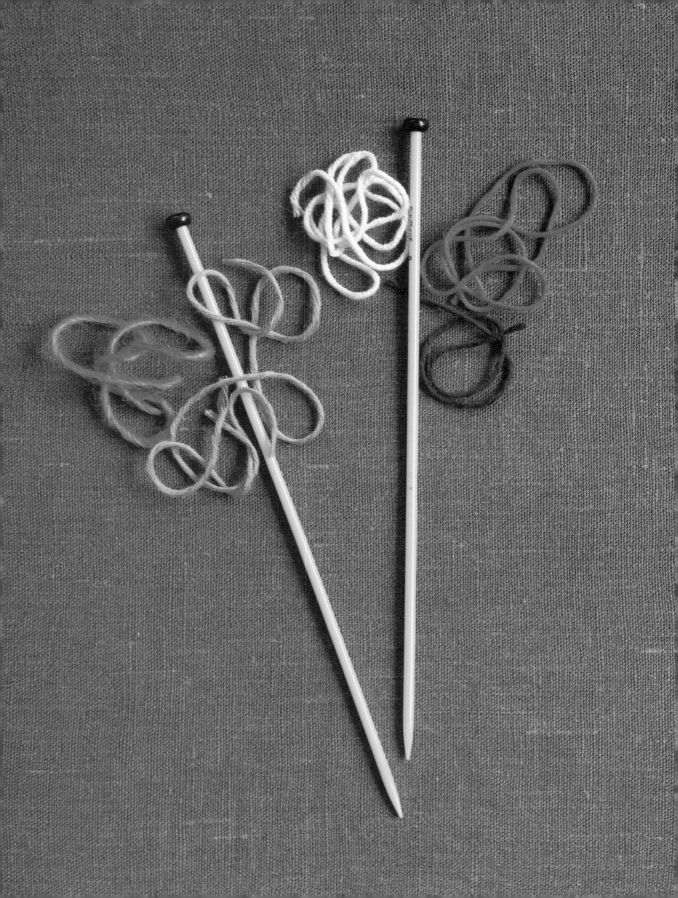

PRETTY PLEASE

I don't need an excuse to make something pretty, and
having had long hair for most of my adult life, I like to
adorn it with knitted fripperies. I hope you are inspired
to experiment by this charming collection of pins and
hairslides decorated with flowers, hearts and pom-poms,
all of which can be mixed and matched. These quick
little projects also make wonderful homemade presents
if you feel so inclined.

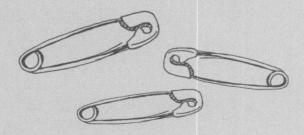

DAHLIA & POPPY CORSAGES

These gorgeous knitted flowers are an ideal way of using up all your small scraps of yarn. The finished flowers can be attached to a brooch or safety pin to make a woolly corsage, or they can be sewn directly on to clothes. If you're feeling a little more extravagant, try knitting 'bunches' of flowers and then sew them together to make a large corsage.

The dahlia has 30 petals and uses garter stitch, casting on and casting/binding off stitches only. The poppy has a few decrease abbreviations in the pattern (which are much easier than they sound) as well as garter stitch.

The flowers shown were knitted using DK (sport-weight) cotton, but you can follow the same pattern and produce different-sized flowers by using a different thickness of yarn (and the appropriate needles, of course): finer yarn will make smaller flowers; thicker yarn will make larger ones.

VARIATION 1: DAHLIA BROOCH

YOU WILL NEED

About 10 g (½ oz) of any DK cotton yarn in your main colour (A) and a scrap of a contrasting yarn (B) for the centre

Pair of 3.25 mm (US 3) knitting needles

Tapestry needle

TENSION/GAUGE

Not important but use smaller needles for a tighter curl.

FINISHED SIZE

Diameter approximately 9cm (3½ in)

LEVEL

Moving on

METHOD

With 3.25 mm (US 3) needles and A.
Row 1: Cast on 18 sts, cast/bind off 14 sts, K to end. (4 sts)
Row 2: K4, turn, cast on 14 sts, cast/bind off 14 sts, K to end.
Row 3: K4, turn, cast on 12 sts, cast/bind off 12 sts, K to end.
Row 4: As Row 2.
Rep Rows 2–4 six times more.
Rows 23–30: As Row 3.
Cast/bind off 4 sts. Leave an end.
Thread a tapestry needle with the yarn from the cast/bound-off end. Coil the knitting around, stitching it tog along the straight edge to secure. Sew in any loose ends.

Flower centre

With 3.25 mm (US 3) needles and B cast on 8 sts. Cast/bind off, leaving a tail, and thread through a tapestry needle.

To finish

Coil the flower centre and stitch through to secure. Using the same thread, pull through the centre of the flower and secure it at the base on the underside. Attach the flower to a brooch pin or a large safety pin with overstitch. Alternatively, attach the flower to a hair grip using overstitch along one edge of the clip only.

VARIATION 2: POPPY HAIR PIN

YOU WILL NEED

For the petals

About 10 g (½ oz) each of any DK cotton in red (A) and navy blue (B); scrap of a contrasting colour for the centre

Pair of 3.25 mm (US 10) knitting needles

Tapestry needle

For the leaf

About 5 g (¼ oz) of any DK cotton yarn

Pair of 3.25 mm (US 3) knitting needles

TENSION/GAUGE

Not important but use smaller needles for stiffer petals.

FINISHED SIZE

7 cm (2¾ in) diameter

LEVEL

Moving on

METHOD

Make four petals.
With 3.25 mm (US 3) and A cast on 5 sts.
Row 1 (RS): Knit.
Row 2: Kfb, K to last 2 sts, Kfb, K1. (7 sts)
Row 3: As Row 2. (9 sts)
Row 4: As Row 2. (11 sts)
Rows 5–8: Knit.
Row 9: Ssk twice, K to last 4 sts, K2tog twice. (7 sts)
Rows 10–12: Knit.
Row 13: Change to B, ssk twice, K2tog, K1. (4 sts)
Row 14–16: Knit.

Row 17: K1, K2tog, K1. (3 sts)
Cast/bind off.
Sew in any loose ends. Place the cast/bound-off edge of two petals together and stitch along this edge, joining the two pieces together. Rep with the other two petals, and place these over the first two to form a cross of four petals. Stitch through the centre. Work a running stitch around all petals on the back at the point where colours A and B meet and gently draw up to make the petals cup slightly.

Centre

With any contrast colour, cast on 10 sts. Cast/bind off 10 sts. Coil this piece up and stitch through, then attach to the centre of the poppy.
Sew in any loose ends. Sew the poppy to a brooch pin, hair clip or safety pin.

Leaf

With 3.25 mm (US 3) needles cast on 12 sts
Rows 1–10: Knit.
Row 11: K4, sl2Kpo, K2tog, K3. (9 sts)
Row 12: K3, sl2Kpo, K2tog, K1. (6 sts)
Row 13: Knit.
Row 14: K1, sl2Kpo, K2tog. (3 sts)
Row 15: K1, K2tog. (2 sts)
Cast/bind off.

Fold the beg and end point of the cast-on edge to the centre to make a leaf shape and stitch in place. Sew in any loose ends. Attach the leaf to the back of the flower.

As a child I had very long hair, and I still have the tartan ribbons from when I wore plaits to school. In my teens and early twenties I cut my hair short – sometimes very short – but since then I have grown it out and have had long hair again for many years. I have a huge collection of hair clips, slides and other hair accessories, and I often wear a flower in my hair. This pattern is my own version of the many silk-style fake flowers I own.

This pattern will work with any yarn. A finer yarn will make a smaller petal and thicker yarn a larger petal, you could also try knitting the petals in different colours or add a leaf or two (see page 110 for instructions).

YOU WILL NEED

About 2 g (scrap) each of Debbie Bliss Eco Aran in Peach (A) and Green (B)

Pair of 3.25 mm (US 3) knitting needles

Tapestry needle

TENSION/GAUGE

Using 3.25 mm (US 3) needles and working in st st, 25 sts and 34 rows = 10 cm (4 in) square

FINISHED SIZE

Each petal 4 cm (1½ in) long and 3.5 cm (1¼ in) at widest point

LEVEL

Moving on

METHOD

Make five petals.
With 3.25 mm (US 3) needles and A cast on 2 sts.
Row 1: K, inc in both sts. (4 sts)
Row 2: Purl.
Row 3: Inc in first st, K2, inc in last st. (6 sts)
Row 4: Purl.
Row 5: Inc in first 2 sts, K2, inc in last 2 sts. (10 sts)
Row 6: Purl.
Row 7: Knit.
Row 8: Purl.
Row 9: Inc in first st, K8, inc in last st. (12 sts)
Row 10: Purl.
Row 11: K2tog 6 times. (6 sts)
Row 12: Purl.
Row 13: K2tog 3 times. (3 sts)
Cut the yarn, leaving an end of about 10 cm (4 in). Keep the 3 sts on the needle until all 5 petals are complete, giving 15 on your needle.
When all the petals are complete, cut the yarn to about 20 cm (8 in) and use a tapestry needle to thread it back

through the 15 sts. Pull it up tight, then thread it through a second time. Using the shorter ends, sew each petal to the adjacent petal about 1 cm (½ in) up the sides from the centre. Tie in any ends.
When the flower is complete use another length of thread to work running stitch around the back of the petals about 1 cm (½ in) from the flower's centre, working a small catch stitch through the centre of each petal once. Gently pull the thread to form the petals into a slight cup. Fasten off.

Centre

With 3.25 mm (US 3) needles and B cast on 15 sts. Cast/bind off 15 sts and cut the yarn, leaving about 15 cm (6 in). Thread it through the last st. Coil this piece around to make the button centre and sew securely in place.

To finish

Using overstitch and sewing thread, attach a kirby (hair) grip to the back of the flower, sewing at the rounded end and halfway down the straight edge of the grip. Fasten off.

this May thanis + Plum X

POM-POM NECKTIE

I was keen to make a contemporary accessory, and coming across some beautiful silk and alpaca yarn inspired me to design this necktie. Very easy to make yet effortlessly stylish, it looks great with a classic little black dress. You can wrap it around your neck like a scarf, leaving the ends to hang loose, tie it into a bow or even wear it as a belt, knotted low on the hip. I placed the small pom-poms on the ends as this strikes me as the most flexible option, but my daughter Martha wants her version to have one large and one small pom-pom placed next to each other halfway along the length of the tie, so that she can wrap it around her neck like a knitted choker.

For a completely different look, you could also make this necktie in a single shade, or choose more subdued colours or a fancier yarn – a mohair yarn with a hint of glitter would work very well for this design, too.

YOU WILL NEED

1 × 50 g (1¾ oz) skein of Debbie Bliss Andes in Gold (A); 1 × 50 g (1¾ oz) skein in Fuchsia (B)

Pair of 4 mm (US 6) knitting needles

TENSION/GAUGE

Using 4 mm (US 6) needles and working in rib, 35 sts and 26 rows = 10 cm (4 in) square

FINISHED SIZE

126 × 4 cm (50 × 1½ in), without stretch including pom-poms

LEVEL

Starting out

METHOD

With 4 mm (US 6) needles and A cast on 14 sts.
Row 1: K1, P1.
Row 2: K1, P1.
Rep Rows 1–2 until work measures 108 cm (42½ in).
Cast/bind off.

Make 2 pom-poms using a 9 cm (3½ in) circle (or your preferred size) and B (see page 74). Leave a long end when tying off the pom-poms. Fold the strip in half and use the yarn from each pom-pom to attach it to each end of the strip. Sew in any loose ends.

HEART PATCH

Over the years, I worked on a number of projects with my dear friend Elspeth Thompson, sadly no longer with us. Writing books together was a lovely addition to a long friendship. While working on a book about things you can make yourself, from cushion covers to Christmas tree decorations, we got talking about patching: Elspeth wanted to start a campaign, 'Bring back the patch', in homage to our teenage years and also as a solution to the dreaded clothes moth. So it is with this conversation in mind that I have made this knitted heart, a patch in the spirit of the late 1970s but also in memory of dear Els. Use it to cover a little hole or sew it to a safety pin so you can use it wherever you need it – pin it to the lapel of your jacket or attach it to a canvas shopping bag.

As with many of these simple little projects, tension/gauge doesn't matter with this pattern, so you can follow the same instructions using any kind of yarn, selecting your needle size as appropriate, to create hearts in a variety of sizes.

YOU WILL NEED

2 g (scrap) of Debbie Bliss Eco Aran in the colour of your choice

Pair of 3.25 mm (US 3) knitting needles; double-pointed needle (dpn)

TENSION/GAUGE

Using 3.25 mm (US 3) needles and working in st st, 25 sts and 34 rows = 10 cm (4 in) square

FINISHED SIZE

4 cm (1½ in) long × 4.5 cm (1¾ in) at the widest point

LEVEL

Starting out

METHOD

With 3.25 mm (US 3) needles cast on 2 sts.

Row 1: K, inc in both sts. (4 sts)

Row 2: Purl.

Row 3: Inc in first st, K2, inc in last st. (6 sts)

Row 4: Purl.

Row 5: Inc in first 2 sts, K2, inc in last 2 sts. (10 sts)

Row 6: Purl.

Row 7: Inc in first st, K8, inc in last st. (12 sts)

Row 8: Purl.

Rows 9–12: Work in st st.

Row 13: K2tog, K2, K2tog. (4 sts)

Turn, keeping other 6 sts on a dpn.

Row 14: Purl.

Row 15: Cast/bind off 4 sts.

Rep Rows 13–15 on rem 6 sts.

Sew in any loose ends.

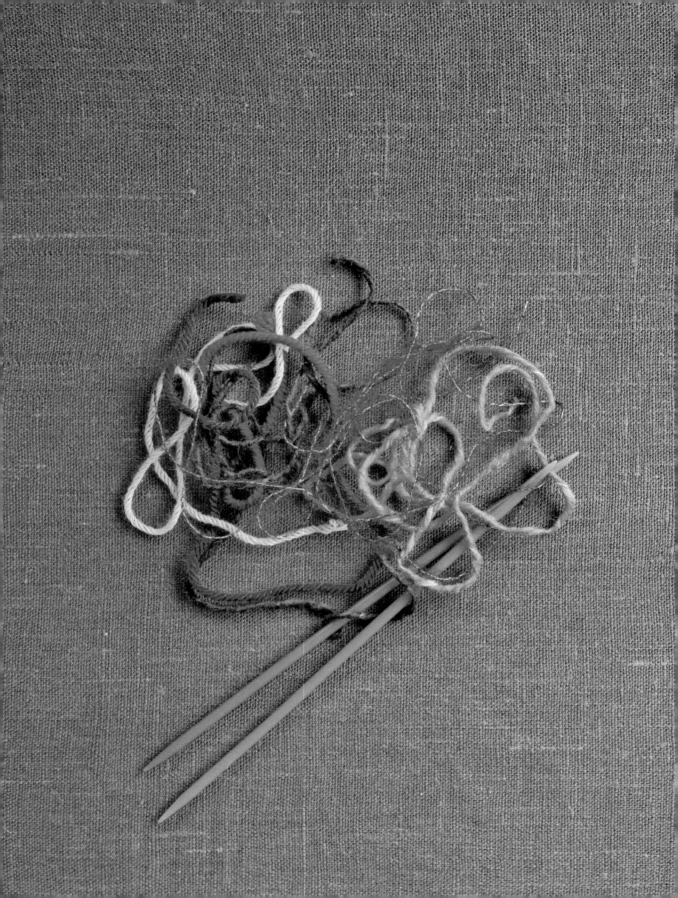

CARRY ME

My daughters and I have a bag for every occasion, and
while this tendency drives my husband a bit dotty, I think
it's very practical to have suitable carry cases for a variety
of different items, from jewellery to a tablet computer.
I love this selection of portable projects, particularly
the sparkly purse with its vintage fabric lining, but my
absolute favourite has to be the dog coat – everyone
needs a cover for when it's chilly.

PRETTY PURSE

I recently found a shabby 1970s fabric purse with a metal clasp. Then as now fashion was influenced by the styles of the 1930s and '40s, so I decided to re-invent this purse for today by attaching the clasp to a piece of knitting instead. I chose a gorgeous mohair yarn with subtle silver filaments to make this glamorous little bag that works as well in the daytime as the evening.

If you can't find an old clasp to repurpose, you can buy similar ones from craft supply stores or online auction sites. Just make sure the clasp has holes punched around the top inside edges so that you can sew your knitting into place: use running stitch, let the holes in the clasp guide you and it will look neat.

I lined my knitting with a piece of silk fabric that started life as a scarf. It had frayed at the edges, but as I can never bear to throw away beautiful fabrics, I put it into my scrap box. A perfect match to the mohair, it has now been transformed from something old into something new, so this project adheres to my favoured mantra: reduce, reuse, recyle.

YOU WILL NEED

1 × 50 g (1¾ oz) ball of Debbie Bliss Party Angel in Midnight/Silver

Pair of 3.25 mm (US 3) and pair of 4 mm (US 6) knitting needles

18 cm (7 in) purse clasp

About 36 × 24 cm (14 × 9½ in) lining fabric

TENSION/GAUGE

Using 4 mm (US 6) needles and working in st st, 22 sts and 32 rows = 10 cm (4 in) square

FINISHED SIZE

22 × 17 cm (8½ × 6½ in); depth when halved

LEVEL

Moving on

TIP

I marked the centre of my work and attached the top of my knitting to the top of the clasp before I stitched the side seams.

METHOD

With 3.25 mm (US 3) needles cast on 50 sts.
Work 4 cm (1½ in) in st st.
Change to 4 mm (US 6) needles and cont in st st until work measures 30 cm (12 in). Change to 3.25 mm (US 3) needles and cont in st st for 4 cm (1½ in) more.
Cast/bind off.

To finish

Fold work in half, RS to RS. Using the clasp as a marker, pin the side seams from the bottom edge to where the edge of clasp will be attached. Sew the side seams to the pinned point. Turn to the RS and sew the knitting to the clasp with running stitch. Secure any ends.

Lining

Fold the lining fabric in half, RS to RS, and mark the point where the clasp will meet the side seams. Stitch the side seams to this point.
With WS to WS fold over the top edge and sides by 1 cm (½ in). Press with an iron. With RS to RS, place the lining inside the knitted purse and pin the folded edge of the lining to the knitting along the top edge, just beneath the clasp, and down both sides. Stitch in place with a small catch stitch.

I have always liked fabric bags, from the tapestry evening bags I have picked up over the years in vintage shops and flea markets to the vintage sewing bags in which I keep my knitting. As a designer and maker, I have designed crochet bags and knitted rucksacks for my children's wear company, Little Badger, as well as knitted bags for fashion designers such as Margaret Howell.

I found a pair of round wooden handles on an old bag, removed the fabric and then designed a bag to go with the handles. As with the clasp on page 120, you can buy a variety of handles in haberdashery stores or online. Knitted in chunky wool, this project grows quickly, and there is no shaping in the actual knitting: once the seams are sewn up, the bag takes its shape from the circular handles.

If you can sew, I recommend making a fabric lining for this bag. Easy to make, the lining not only adds a gorgeous finishing touch to this project – I used a vintage floral fabric that flashes its lovely colours when the bag is in use – but it also helps the bag keep its shape. You can of course make this bag without a lining, but you may find that it 'grows' with the weight of its contents.

YOU WILL NEED

4 × 50 g (1¾ oz) balls of Debbie Bliss Rialto Chunky in Ruby

Pair of 6.5 mm (US 10½) knitting needles

2 × 14 cm (5½ in) diameter wooden circular handles (any shape would work)

About 85 × 80 cm (33½ × 31½ in) lining fabric (optional; I used a piece of vintage chintz)

TENSION/GAUGE

Using 6.5 mm (US 10½) needles and working in st st, 14 sts and 20 rows = 10 cm (4 in) square

FINISHED SIZE

About 41 × 36.5 cm (16¼ × 14½ in)

LEVEL

Moving on

METHOD

With 6.5 mm (US 10½) needles cast on 57 sts.

Row 1 (WS): Purl.
Row 2: P1, [K1, P1] to end.
Row 3 (and all WS rows): Purl.
Rows 4, 8 and 12: Knit.
Rows 6 and 10: P1, [K7, P1] to end.

Rep Rows 1–12 twelve times more, then work Rows 1–3 again. Cast/bind off.

To finish

Fold the knitting in half, RS to RS and with cast-on edge to cast-off (bound-off) edge. Sew the side seams together, matching the pattern and beg sewing at folded edge up to 20 cm (8 in) from the top edge.

On both sides, with RS still facing, flatten out the work so that the seam is at the centre. Take a corner to about 6 cm (2½ in) along the folded edge. Pin in position, then sew across the corner with backstitch. Rep with the other corner. Turn the right way out. The bag will now have a shaped base.

Fold the top edges over the wooden handles and pin in place. Sew neatly with overstitch.

Lining

Cut 2 pieces of lining fabric, each 41 × 35 cm (13¾ × 14½ in). Sew the bottom seam. Sew both side seams to 12 cm (4¾ in) from the top edge.

Put the lining into the knitted bag. Pin in place along the edges of the side splits and turn the top edges of lining in along the top edges below the channel that holds the handles. Sew into place with a neat overstitch.

WAVY DOLLY BAG

I love the looks you can achieve with this chevron stitch, especially when it's knitted in stripes: changing colour every four rows creates a wonderful wavy effect. By using extra-fine lacy yarn, as I have here, you can make a beautiful piece of work that could easily be mistaken for a piece of vintage knitting from the 1920s or '30s, which is what I set out to achieve with this design.

This simple but striking pattern is worked over four rows, and requires you to get the hang of the 'knit two together' (K2tog) and 'pass slip stitch over' (psso) techniques (see pages 24–25). As with many of the patterns in this book, you could follow the same instructions using a thicker yarn, changing needle size as appropriate, to make a larger bag. Instead of the drawstring closure, you could also attach your work to small wooden handles to make an evening bag – simply follow the instructions for the tote bag on page 122.

YOU WILL NEED

Total weight 20 g (¾ oz) of Debbie Bliss Rialto Lace in Sage (A), Sky (B), Gold (C), Lilac (D) and Stone (E)

Pair of 2.75 mm (US 2) knitting needles

TENSION/GAUGE

Using 2.75 mm (US 2) needles and working in st st, 33 sts and 50 rows = 10 cm (4 in); the row tension/gauge will vary from knitter to knitter

FINISHED SIZE

15 cm (6 in) long and 12 cm (5¾ in) wide

LEVEL

Going further

TIP

This is a great pattern for using up small ends of yarn.

METHOD

Make two.
With 2.75 mm (US 2) needles and E cast on 52 sts.
Work 8 rows in st st.
Work 2 rows st st in each colour as foll: D, C, B and A (16 rows in all).
Change to E and work in patt as foll:
Row 1: *Inc 1 (K into front and back of st), K4, sl1, K2tog, psso, K4, inc 1 (as before)*, rep from * to * to end.
Row 2: Purl.
Row 3: As Row 1.
Row 4: Knit.
Change to D and rep Rows 1–4.
Change to C and rep Rows 1–4.
Change to B and rep Rows 1–4.
Change to A and rep Rows 1–4.
Rep last 20 rows twice more then cast/bind off.

To finish

Stitch the cast-on edge to the 16th row from the edge with a neat overstitch to make a channel. With RS to RS, sew the cast-off (bound-off) edge of one piece to the cast-off (bound-off) edge of second piece. Sew the side seams from the base edge to the channel.
Use D to make 2 × 44 cm (17 in) twisted cords (see page 74). Thread one cord through both channels and tie the ends together with a double knot. Rep with the second cord, but beg threading from the opposite side. Pull up the cords to create the drawstring.

DOG COAT

I grew up with dogs but have only ever had cats in my own house. I would love to have a dog one day, and when my daughters leave home … who knows! But in the meantime, I am forever on the website of the Battersea Dogs & Cats Home, looking for potential strays I could take in. I'm also very fond of a number of friends' dogs.

Living in a city means that most of my friends have smaller dogs and I have learned that they often need a little help keeping warm when out for a walk on a winter's day. This little coat is another fairly easy project: the tweedy yarn makes it look sophisticated but it is made mostly using garter stitch, so there is nothing much to it. The optional trim involves a crochet chain stitch, but your dog would be just as happy wearing a plain coat. This is a one-size pattern, so if you want to make a coat for a larger dog, I would suggest you try knitting it in a chunkier yarn, or you could add extra stitches when casting on and adjust the pattern accordingly for length.

YOU WILL NEED

2 × 50 g (1¾ oz) balls of Debbie Bliss Luxury Tweed Aran in Forest (A); 1 × 50 g (1¾ oz) in Tangerine (B)

Pair of 5 mm (US 8) and pair of 4 mm (US 6) knitting needles

Stitch holder

4.5 mm (US 7) crochet hook

TENSION/GAUGE

Using 5 mm (US 8) needles and working in st st, 18 sts and 24 rows = 10 cm (4 in) square

FINISHED SIZE

40 cm (15¾ in) long × 26 cm (10¼ in) wide at widest point when flat

LEVEL

Going further

TIP

If you do not use a contrasting colour you will need only 2 balls of yarn.

PROJECT…

METHOD

With 4 mm (US 6) needles and B cast on 65 sts.
Work 1 row in K1, P1 rib. Change to A and cont in rib for
10 cm (4 in). Note that alt rows start with P1.
Change to 5 mm (US 8) needles and work 3 cm (1¼ in)
in garter st (knit every row).
Next row: K41, keep rem 24 sts on a stitch holder.
Turn and cont on 41 sts, mark each end of last row with
a contrast thread, working in garter st until the piece
measures 36 cm (14 in) from the cast-on edge.
Beg shaping as foll:
Next row: K2, K2tog, K to last 4 sts, K2tog, K2. (39 sts)
Rep last row until 9 sts rem.
Next row: K2tog, K2tog, K1, K2tog, K2tog. (5 sts)
Next row: K2tog, K1, K2tog. (3 sts)
Cast/bind off.
Pick up 24 sts from the stitch holder and work in garter st
for 14 cm (5½ in). Cast/bind off in B.

Edging (optional)

With a 4.5 mm (US 7) crochet hook and B used double
and with RS facing, beg and end between markers, work
a chain stitch all around the edge of the main body of
work, inserting the hook between each ridge of the sides
and between each row on the dec section.

To finish

Join seam from cast-on edge to marker. Stitch
underneath flap to the main body sides for about 3 cm
(1¼ in) from cast/bound-off edge leaving gaps for legs
to pass through.

When it comes to being more environmentally aware, a little effort can go a long way. Refusing plastic bags when you are shopping and bringing your own string bag instead is one such simple measure. Not only will you be able to reuse the bag again and again, you will have the added satisfaction of being able to say 'I made this myself!'

This design is practical, efficient and light but you will be surprised at how much this bag will hold, and the long straps mean you can carry it over your shoulder. You can make a selection in different colours – they will look very attractive hanging together on the back of the door – or you could even use one in the kitchen to store your vegetables.

The lace pattern is satisfying to knit and grows very quickly. I would advise buying yarn on a cone for this project so that you don't have to sew in any loose ends when you finish the bag. You could opt for a shorter bag by knitting fewer rows or you may prefer to make shorter handles – as with opting to 'go green', it is all a matter of choice.

YOU WILL NEED

150 g (5 oz) of Yeoman Yarn DK Cotton in Yellow; if possible use DK (sport-weight) cotton yarn from a cone to avoid having to sew in any ends over the cat's eye stitch

Pair of 3.5 mm (US 4) knitting needles

3.5 mm (US 4) and 8 mm (US 11) circular needles

TENSION/GAUGE

Using 3.5 mm (US 4) needles and working in garter st, 20 sts and 40 rows = 10 cm (4 in) square

FINISHED SIZE

Depending on the stretch, about 40 cm (15¾ in) wide × 34 cm (13½ in) deep; these measurements are approximate because it is difficult to measure accurately over this loose stitch

LEVEL

Moving on

METHOD

Make two.

Leaving a 100 cm (40 in) end and with 3.5 mm (US 4) needles cast on 40 sts.

Knit 20 rows in garter stitch (knit every row).

Next row: K1, [M1, K2] to last st, M1, K1. (60 sts)

Next row: Change to an 8 mm (US 11) circular needle and knit.

Cont working 'cat's eye' stitch as foll:

Row 1: P2, [yo, P4tog] to last 2 sts, P2.

Row 2: K2, *K1, (K1, P1, K1) into st made on the previous row*, rep from * to * to last 2 sts, K2.

Row 3: Knit.

Rep Rows 1–3 14 times (or fewer for a shorter bag).

On last patt for Rows 2 and 3 of the patt change to a 3.5 mm (US 4) circular needle. (60 sts)

Next row: Knit.

Cast on 100 sts, inserting the needle through 2 sts for the first st for added strength. Make sure that the cast-on st is not twisted, then join into a round for the handle.

Round 1: Purl (to simulate knit).

Change to knit when you come back on the cast-on sts. This marks the beg of each round. K2tog when you reach the other end of the cast-on sts to cover the inevitable gap.

Next round: Purl.

Next round: Knit.

Rep last 2 rounds 4 times more on each side of the handle, but on the last purl round dec over the 60 sts of the bag part, [P5, P2tog] 8 times, P4, then cast/bind off loosely over the handle but as tightly as you can over the 'bag' section.

Leave at least 100 cm (about 40 in) of yarn after finishing casting/binding off. Thread it down through the sts of the handle and leave until later.

To finish

Starting from the original cast-on edge, use the whole length of thread to join the short ends of the garter st panels as neatly as possible. Work an overstitch before you start on the openwork, then pick up stitches from alt sides (no backstitching) until you reach about 9 cm (3½ in) from the top. Stretch the seam as far as you can to keep an even tension/gauge. Work several overstitches to secure the top of the seam. Rep on the opposite side. When you have completed both sides turn the bag inside out and join the cast-on edges together stitch for stitch, leaving a 20 cm (8 in) length at the start of the seam and a similar length when you finish.

Turn back to the RS, bring both threads to the outside and tie them together (this pulls both corners together). Mark the centre of the seam, flatten out the points and stitch them firmly to the centre of the base of bag. Using the thread double, stitch three or four times (see the photograph). Sew in the ends to the WS and finish off.

Variation

To reinforce the open sides of the bag you could blanket stitch the 9 cm (3½ in) length from the top of the side seam to the garter stitch handles on all four sides.

COFFEE COSY

This playful little project is really a bit of frippery but it is surprisingly practical. Inspired by the cardboard sleeves that come with most take-away hot drinks these days, I first thought of it as a way to use up short ends of yarn. Make one of these to keep in your bag and you will be able to feel smug about refusing the disposable version and not contributing to yet more landfill. This design is a doddle to knit as it only uses garter stitch, and the best thing about it is that it actually works! This woolly sleeve saves you from burning your fingers on the cup, keeps your drink hotter for longer and doubles as a hand warmer.

This design is so small and simple you will have it knitted in a trice. It's the perfect starter project for a beginner: you could wangle some ends of yarn from a knitting friend, as you will only need 5 grams (¼ oz) each of three different colours. You could make it even simpler by using 15 grams (½ oz) of a single colour instead of knitting stripes, or if you only have very small amounts of yarn, you could make it using lots of different colours.

YOU WILL NEED

About 5 g (¼ oz) of Debbie Bliss Cashmerino Aran in each of Teal (A), Lime (B) and Charcoal (C)

Pair of 5 mm (US 8) knitting needles

TENSION/GAUGE

Using 5 mm (US 8) needles and working in garter st, 18 sts and 40 rows = 10 cm (4 in) square

FINISHED SIZE

9.5 × 7 cm (3¾ × 2¾ in) flat, 19 cm (7½ in) all around

LEVEL

Starting out

METHOD

With 5 mm (US 8) needles and A cast on 34 sts.

Row 1: Knit.
Row 2: Knit.
Change to B.
Rep Rows 1–2.
Change to C.
Rep Rows 1–2.
Rep the last 6 rows 3 times more.
Change to A.
Row 25: Knit.
Row 26: Knit.
Cast/bind off knitwise.
Sew the side seam and weave in any loose ends.

TABLET COVER

Technology has taken over most of our lives, with laptops, smart phones, e-readers and tablet computers being everyday items in many households. As we frequently carry them around with us, these costly mobile devices need to be protected, which adds yet another expense, so a homemade cover is a wonderful option. I knitted this one using a textured stripe, with two vintage buttons to fasten it, and think it would make a perfect present.

Once you have a good understanding of how knitting tensions/gauges work you could adapt the pattern to fit a device of any size: measure the item and use a tension/gauge square (see page 35) to figure out how many stitches you will need to knit a piece of the appropriate width. Cast on that amount, then knit until your work is long enough to form an envelope.

YOU WILL NEED

2 × 50 g (1¾ oz) balls of Debbie Bliss Cashmerino Aran in Blackberry

Pair of 5 mm (US 8) knitting needles

2 × vintage buttons

TENSION/GAUGE

Using 5 mm (US 8) needles and working in st st, 18 sts and 26 rows = 10 cm (4 in) square

FINISHED SIZE

21 × 25 cm (8¼ × 20 in)

LEVEL

Moving on

METHOD

With 5 mm (US 8) needles cast on 36 sts and work 2 cm (¾ in) in garter st (knit every row).
Then work as foll:
Row 1 (RS): Knit.
Row 2: Purl.
Row 3: Knit.
Row 4: Purl.
Row 5: Knit.
Row 6: Knit.
Row 7: Knit.
Row 8: Purl.
Row 9: Knit.
Row 10: Purl.
Row 11: Knit.
Row 12: Knit.
Row 13: Purl.
Row 14: Knit.
Rep Rows 1–14 eight times more.
Begin flap.
Next row: As Row 1.

Next row: K4, P to last 4 sts, K4.
Next row: As Row 3.
Next row: K4, P to last 4 sts, K4.
Rep Rows 5–7 as above.
Row 8: K4, P to last 4, K4.
Row 9: K6, cast/bind off 2 sts, K to last 8 sts, cast/bind off 2 sts, K to end.
Row 10: K4, P2, , cast on 1 st, P to last 6 sts, cast on 1 st, P2, K4.
Row 11: K6, *K1 on cast-on (bound-on) thread, then pick up and knit another 1 on same thread, K to last 7 sts*, rep from * to *, K6. This will make a neat buttonhole.
Work 5 rows more in garter st.
Cast/bind off.

To finish

Position cast-on edge of cover in line with beginning of flap. Sew side seams. Sew on buttons to correspond with buttonholes.

YARNS USED IN THIS BOOK

Designer Yarns for Debbie Bliss yarn (among others) were incredibly helpful supplying yarn for the projects in this book and I would highly recommend them.
www.designeryarns.uk.com
Unit 8–10 Newbridge Industrial Estate, Pitt Street, Keighley, West Yorkshire BD21 4PQ
Tel: 01535 664222

Debbie Bliss
www.debbieblissonline.com
Debbie is a brilliant knitwear designer and her yarn range reflects her style – fabulous colours.

Erika Knight
www.erikaknight.co.uk
The lovely Erika Knight has produced a new yarn range that I would have included had it been available in time. Sadly not, but I will next time.

Yeoman Yarns
www.yeoman-yarns.co.uk
36 Churchill Way, Fleckney, Leicestershire LE8 8UD
Tel: 0116 2404464
I have used Yeoman yarns for over 25 years for commercial and personal work. They stock the perfect mercerised cotton 'Canelle' that I would be lost without.

FAVOURITE YARN SHOPS

Loop
www.loopknitting.com
5 Camden Passage, Islington, London N1 8EA
A visit to Loop is always inspiring and is a must for all knitters. The shop is very stylish with a great range of stock and the staff are hugely helpful and well informed.

I Knit London
www.iknit.org.uk
106 Lower Marsh, Waterloo, London SE1 7AB | Tel: 020 7261 1338
This quirky shop is well worth a visit, I love it.

Moo Too
45 Lordship Lane, East Dulwich, London SE22 8EP
Tel: 020 8299 6105
Local to me, the wool and haberdashery area in this shop is developing fast.

Sharp Works
www.sharpworks.co.uk
220 Railton Road, Herne Hill, London SE24 0JT | Tel: 020 7738 7668
I am very lucky to have such a well-stocked wool shop a five-minute walk away, run by an extremely helpful mother and daughter team. They also run workshops.

MORE GREAT YARN SHOPS

These have been recommended by my followers. I have looked at their websites and think they all look great.

UK
Stag and Bow
www.stagandbow.com
8 Dartmouth Road, Forest Hill, London SE23 3XU
Tel: 020 8291 4992

Knit With Attitude
www.knitwithattitude.com
127 Stoke Newington High Street, London N16 0PH

Nest
www.handmadenest.co.uk
102 Weston Park, Crouch End, London N8 9PP | Tel: 020 8340 8852

Mrs Moon
www.mrsmoon.co.uk
41 Crown Road, St Margarets, London TW1 3EJ | Tel: 020 8744 1190

Bluestocking Wool & Gifts
www.bluestockingwag.com
22 Westward Road, Cainscross, Stroud GL5 4JQ | Tel: 01453 764887

Get Knitted
www.getknitted.com
39 Brislington Hill, Bristol BS4 5BE
0117 3005211

Wool
www.woolbath.co.uk
19 Old Orchard Street, Bath BA1 1JU
Tel: 01225 469144

Kuiama Crafts
www.kuiamacrafts.co.uk
St Ives, Cornwall
Tel: 01736 798 009

Cafe Knit
www.cafeknit.com
46 High Street, Lavenham, Suffolk CO10 9PY | Tel: 01787 249865

Woolpatch Gallery
www.woolpatchgallery.co.uk
Aerial House, Hall Street, Long Melford, Sudbury, Suffolk CO10 9JR
Tel: 01787 313452

The Sheep Shop
www.sheepshopcambridge.co.uk
72 Beche Road, Cambridge CB5 8HU
Tel: 01223 311268

The Little Wool Shop
www.thelittlewoolshop.co.uk
10 Central Arcade, Saffron Walden CB10 1ER

In Stitches
5a Market Street, Llandeilo, Carmarthenshire SA19 6AH
Tel: 01558 822282

Purl City Yarns
www.purlcityyarns.com
62 Port Street, Manchester M1 2EQ
Tel: 0161 425 3864

The Knit Studio
www.theknitstudio.co.uk
Blackfriars, 6 Friars Green, Newcastle upon Tyne NE1 4XN

The Wool Baa
www.thewoolbaa.co.uk
83 Junction Road, Sheffield S11 8XA
Tel: 0114 266 6262

Tangled Yarn
www.tangled-yarn.co.uk
100 Compstall Road, Romiley,
Stockport SK6 4DE
Tel: 0161 494 2053

The Knitting Parlour
www.theknittingparlour.co.uk
12 Graham Road, Great Malvern,
Worcs WR14 2HN
Tel: 01684 892079

Marmalade yarns
www.marmaladeyarns.co.uk
11 Catherine Hill, Frome, Somerset
BA11 1BZ
Tel: 01373 473557

Old Maiden Aunt Yarns
www.oldmaidenaunt.com
Studio 30, Ritchie Street, West
Kilbride KA23 9AL

USA
Purl Soho
www.purlsoho.com
459 Broome Street New York,
NY 10013 | Tel: (212) 420 8796

Knitty City
www.knittycity.com
208 W. 79th St. New York, NY, 10024
Tel: (212) 787 5896

Downtown Yarns
www.downtownyarns.com
45 Avenue A, New York 10009
Tel: (212) 995 5991

Paradise Fibers
www.paradisefibers.com
225 W Indiana, Spokane WA 99205
Tel: (888) 320 7746

THE BIG BOYS

Texere
www.texere-yarns.co.uk

Jamiesons of Shetland
www.jamiesonsofshetland.co.uk

Deramores
www.deramores.com

Liberty
www.liberty.co.uk

John Lewis Partnership
www.johnlewis.com

HABERDASHERY

Wayward
www.wayward.co
68 Norman Road, St. Leonards On
Sea, East Sussex TN38 0EJ
Tel: 07815 013337
This is where I bought the silver
filament for the socks – it is an amazing
resource for vintage haberdashery and
fabric. Andrew has a Saturday stall in
Gardners Street Market, Brighton and
is at Portobello Road Market every
Friday morning, just under the flyover
towards Goldborne Road, very close to
another favourite…

The Cloth Shop
www.theclothshop.net
290 Portobello Road, London
W10 5TE | Tel: 020 8968 6001

Millie Moon
www.milliemoonshop.co.uk
24-25 Catherine Hill, Frome, Somerset
BA11 1BY Tel: 01373 464650
14a Broad Street, Wells, Somerset
BA5 2DN | Tel: 01749 673090

Halfpenny Home
www.halfpennyhome.co.uk
3 Station Yard, Needham Market,
Suffolk IP6 8AS | Tel: 01449 720468

Fabric8
www.fabric8online.co.uk
3–5 Hamilton Road, Felixstowe
IP11 7AX
Tel: 01394 283186
12–14 Head Street, Colchester
CO1 1NY | Tel: 01206 763432

Pinwheel Haberdashery
www.pinwheelhaberdashery.co.uk
377 Stockport Road, Timperley,
Cheshire WA15 7UR
Tel: 07813 052309

Lloyd Waters
www.lloydwaters.co.uk
1a Market Place Great Dunmow Essex
CM6 1A | Tel: 01371 876149

Brighton Sewing Centre
www.brightonsewingcentre.co.uk
68 North Road, Brighton BN1 1YD
Tel: 01273 621 653

Hoop
www. hoophaberdashery.co.uk
92 High Street, Tenterden, Kent
TN30 6JB | Tel: 01580 388011

The Bead Trail
www.thebeadtrail.co.uk
Tel: 01606 559566

WEBSITES

www.abakhan.co.uk
www.cascadeyarns.com
www.laughinghens.com
www.tailormouse.co.uk
www.ravelry.com
www.toroidalsnark.net

FAVOURITE BLOGS

I look at these for general inspiration,
not just for knitting…
ny10536.tumblr.com
ancientindustries.blogspot.co.uk
2or3things.blogspot.co.uk
thewomensroom.typepad.com
justine-picardie.blogspot.co.uk
gardenista.com
silverpebble-jewellery.blogspot.co.uk
lolanovablog.blogspot.co.uk
onechurchillsgreen.typepad.com
purplepoddedpeas.blogspot.co.uk
teenagegranny.blogspot.co.uk
sewrecycled.blogspot.co.uk
krishenkavintagetreasures.blogspot.
co.uk

INDEX

ACKNOWLEDGEMENTS

To publisher Alison Starling at Mitchell Beazley who persisted. To Denise Bates at Octopus who always seems to be around whenever I am fortunate enough to have a book commissioned, and to my agent Jane Turnbull, thank you.

Yuki Sugiura – a brilliant photographer with a wonderful eye for detail – you have taken exceptional pictures. To my friend Cynthia Inions who makes styling seem effortless: how does she do that? To Juliette Norsworthy for her calm, steady eye, the perfect art director, and to Anita Mangan for her wonderful book design and stylish illustrations, your skills are much appreciated. To Kim Lightbody, Yuki's assistant, who added an air of glamour to our shoot, for modelling, making great tea and for being a lovely talented young woman. To Alex and Katy for their editing skills. I am very lucky... Thank you team, you have made this book beautiful.

A huge thank you to Monica McMillan in Aviemore for being the most reliable sample knitter, pattern corrector and sounding board. To my Mum Ruth for helping sample knit yet again and to Marilyn Wilson for her pattern checking.

Thank you 'models' – mainly people who popped in to my house and the one in Brixton while we were shooting! Anna Blair, Chenille Burnham Simpson, Millar Maxwell, Anna Morton, Matthew Newton, Cynthia (again), Kim (again), my lovely daughters Martha & Ce who were roped in (as ever) to appear in the odd shot, and last but not least Charli the Dachshund.

Huge thanks to Debbie Bliss for providing such beautiful yarn via www.designeryarns.co.uk and to Celtic Cove for their prompt deliveries.

To Caddy & Chris for lending us their beautiful house, garden and chickens, to friends here & departed and lastly to Ben Murphy my husband, always there, however vaguely.